Of Women

Of Women

SHAMI CHAKRABARTI

ALLEN LANE
an imprint of
PENGUIN BOOKS

ALLEN LANE

UK | USA | Canada | Ireland | Australia
India | New Zealand | South Africa

Allen Lane is part of the Penguin Random House group of companies
whose addresses can be found at global.penguinrandomhouse.com

First published 2017
001

Extracts from articles by Pharie Sefali (*GroundUp*, 6 November 2014) and
Anthony Loyd (*The Times*, 8 May 2017) are reproduced by permission.

The moral right of the author has been asserted

Set in 13.5/16 pt Garamond MT Std
Typeset by Jouve (UK), Milton Keynes
Printed in Great Britain by Clays Ltd, St Ives plc

A CIP catalogue record for this book is available from the British Library

ISBN: 978–0–241–29634–9

www.greenpenguin.co.uk

For you my darling,
In memory of my mother,
And for the sons and daughters of women everywhere.

Contents

Introduction

It is autumn again. That shouldn't matter and yet somehow it does. We are sophisticated creatures in so many ways, but retain something of the primitive respect for days and years like picture frames or book ends that help us cope with memories, space and time. So the turn of another season inevitably encourages reflection and stock-taking. For some this exercise can be an extremely close and practical one. How tall are the children? How big is the debt? Can we afford the rent; the mortgage? Does the room need a clear-out; the hedge cutting back? And yet the seismic events of recent times would challenge the focus of even the most inward-looking soul. For this is an extraordinary moment. All over the world post-millennial crises in security, the economy and climate have created an appetite for radicalism of different kinds. This brings both enormous challenges and opportunities for progressive values. Will we descend into further nationalism, racism and perennial war? Or will we return instead to hope in international responses to shared global problems? Will rising tides of anger at the ever greater inequality delivered by political elites since the 1980s result in success for popular movements of the left or right? In particular, will the recent resurgence of interest in the women's cause become part of a wider struggle for social justice or fragment into a 'niche' or 'single' issue and be left behind?

The 2017 elections in the Netherlands, France and the UK provide some significant reason for hope. All three ballots saw an ultimate rejection of the hard-right xenophobia of the PVV, Front National and UKIP. The British Labour Party led by Jeremy Corbyn confounded the cynicism of its critics and forced an over-confident right-wing Conservative leadership into minority government. It took women's representation in the House of Commons to its highest-ever proportion, if still only 32 per cent. It delivered a 50 per cent female Shadow Cabinet with Emily Thornberry, Diane Abbott, Nia Griffiths and Rebecca Long-Bailey holding the traditionally male bastion briefs of Foreign and Home Affairs, Defence and Business. Just as important was the positive nature of both the substance and tone of the Labour campaign against austerity and inequality, standing in sharp contrast with the smears, character attacks and dog whistles from the right. However, the 'hung parliament' outcome of the election left the Conservatives limping on in office, if not quite in power, propped up this time by the Northern Irish Democratic Unionist Party, with its reactionary position on women's reproductive rights in particular. The new spotlight on socially conservative forces in UK politics serves as a reminder that no creed or country has a monopoly of virtue as far as the place of women is concerned.

Imagine a Martian falls to earth tonight. Let's say Martians are sexless and completely unaccustomed to sexual or gender-based difference on their own planet. Our alien friend could arrive absolutely anywhere in our world, on any continent, in a rich, poor, urban or rural environment. What difference, discrimination or oppression would they notice everywhere and most of all? Surely they could not fail to observe that roughly half the race is overtly diminished in a way that diminishes the other half in a manner that is perhaps more subtle but nonetheless real. Look at the suicide rates of young men in particular. Look at them all over the world in and out of war, crime and incarceration. Look at your kind, clever and gentle sons, brothers, husbands and lovers, and the pressures that can make them become the closed and invulnerable bullies who first bullied them. Wasted potential. Lost happiness. Wasted life.

I don't want to call the glass half empty but the pace of its filling is certainly too slow. Twenty years ago I thought we were in inevitable positive transition. Fresh from the comfort and confidence of a completely free and relatively egalitarian state higher education, I had all the time in the world and thought I would not need it. Now I am not so sure. At least in the short term. I had so much faith in my generation of similarly educated young men and women who shared classes, books and dreams but grew up to betray each other and themselves, with crunched credit, illegal wars and a more unequal world of our own making. What would a Pankhurst or de Beauvoir make of my generation of feminists? No doubt there would be some cause for celebration but the festivities would surely be muted. Women vote, fight and own property and power in many parts of the world but, whether by hook or by crook, an unbowed misogynist took the keys to the White House from a woman who once seemed a near inevitable first female leader of the 'free world'. And in so many places women learn, earn, influence and govern less and suffer more, whether from the petty but dehumanizing indignities of casual objectification and discrimination, or from the emotional and physical violence that dulls and even snuffs out so many of their lives too soon.

Gender injustice may be the greatest human rights abuse on the planet. It blights first and developing worlds; rich and poor women in the context of health, wealth, education, representation, opportunity and security everywhere. It is no exaggeration to describe it as an 'apartheid', but not limited to one country or historical period. For this ancient and continuing wrong is millennial in duration and global in reach. Only radical solutions can even scratch its surface. However, the prize is a great one because of the enormous collateral benefits to peace, prosperity, sustainability and general human happiness. All this because we are all interconnected and all men are 'Of Women' too.

1. Prayer Before Birth

If you had your time again and had your choice, which sex would you choose? Don't dismiss the question out of hand or deal with it summarily out of loyalty to your now determined and experienced sex. Play along with the thought experiment. Try to be honest. Which would you choose? What criteria would affect your decision? Would your feelings alter depending upon the information at your disposal about where you would be born and in what kind of circumstances? Let me put the question another way. What if you are to have a child? Just one. You want that human being to have the best life chances and actual life possible. You know that so much is uncertain in this world in flux. You want them to have the best possible prospects of being safe, secure, healthy, wealthy and even happy and fulfilled. If you could, which sex would you gift to this precious only child? Would it depend on your class, continent, cultural background or preference for the company and camaraderie of your own sex or the other? Are you influenced by your relationship with either of your own parents? What do you find most affects your choice?

It is now over a quarter of a century since the Nobel Laureate economist Amartya Sen wrote of the one hundred million missing women in the world. He based this revelation on the statistically suspicious imbalance in the number of women and men respectively. How many women are missing still today?

Discrimination begins before birth with the practice of

sex-based abortion, particularly in societies where strides in modern medicine and technology have not been matched by similar progress in the social and economic realities and related cultural attitudes towards having sons and daughters. In many parts of the world, the joy of having a baby boy is still equally matched by the sadness at having a girl child to feed, keep free from pre-marital sex and violence, provide a dowry for and so on. And then, after all that investment and anxiety and if things actually go well and according to custom and plan, the girl will only inevitably be 'lost' to another family, like livestock, in the fullness of time.

A highly educated and successful professional friend from a similarly well-educated and successful Indian family once told me that her grandmother had wept tears of disappointment at the birth of each of her three granddaughters. It is not uncommon for parents with daughters but no sons to receive expressions of kind commiseration from friends and family there. One of many heart-breaking moments in Leslee Udwin's shockingly powerful 2015 film *India's Daughter*, comes when Jyoti Singh's father describes how he and his wife had bucked local trend and given sweets to their neighbours in celebration of the birth of their baby, even though she was a girl. Jyoti grew up to be a loving daughter and hard-working medical student, who was subjected to the most horrific gang-rape and murder at the age of twenty-three.

Sen contrasted the majority female population in Europe, the United States and Japan – explicable by a greater resistance to disease once in receipt of similar nutrition and healthcare to men – with the position in most of Asia and North Africa (though there are of course strong national and regional variations). Here the female majority is reversed by a combination of pre-birth deselection and subsequent gender-biased neglect. But even that kind of discrimination does not account for the sheer scale of the numbers. India and China are countries of particular concern when it comes to the sinister and unnatural disparity in the ratio of men to women.

In the summer of 2016 women's rights activist Rita Baṇerji wrote of a 'female genocide' in India encompassing the infanticide of baby girls, their neglect (for example by under-feeding girls compared to boys when food is short and rationed), and even the deliberate killing of older daughters. Even more shockingly, she described the phenomenon as being exacerbated and not improved by greater wealth in the country as a whole, as well as in particular states and com-munities. She ultimately attributes this counter-intuitive trend to the dowry system which will send more wealth out of a wealthier family that has daughters in favour of those with sons. This creates an incentive towards the neglect and worse of girls. And yet to effectively engineer a deficit in women will inevitably create further problems for women and society down the track. The shortage will lend itself to the objectification of women, even to the point of girls being sold as brides or trafficked as sex slaves, as described in vari-ous sections of the great Sue Lloyd-Roberts's journalistic last will and testament of 2016, *The War on Women*.

In some East African cultures, for example, a shortage of women arises as a result of the practice of polygamy, popular among societies in Kenya, Tanzania and South Sudan. Here, girls and women will effectively be bought by a groom's fam-ily for a 'bride price' rather than let go by their own families with the sweetener of a dowry. In these communities, the bride price is paid in recognition of the opportunity cost to the girl's kin in terms of lost monetary earnings, domestic or agricultural labour and that of the children she will produce.

Nonetheless, whether a bride is sold as an asset or taken on as a liability for a fee, the result remains the commodification of girls and women rather than any great appreciation of their real human worth. Further, a shortage of and higher demand for females, far from protecting or improving their status and safety as some have argued, instead makes them more vulnerable to being acquired, even as child brides or kidnapped.

The Indian state of Kerala is a particularly interesting case study for both Sen in 1990 and Banerji in 2016. It is well known for both its matrilineal and communist history, and Sen described it as having one of the best ratios of women to men on the subcontinent. But twenty-six years later, Banerji wrote of that positive ratio, which had always been attributed to a very high literacy rate, plunging by 8.44 per cent by 2011 to coincide with reports of 'rampant foeticide and infanticide' and a large influx of money from Indians working abroad. Banerji explains the reason for the strange trend:

> The answer is dowry – the insidious, misogynist, patriarchal politics of wealth ownership and distribution. The more wealth a family accrues, the more invested it becomes in the patriarchal retention of that wealth and views daughters as a threat to that goal.

It is widely believed that the one-child policy that operated in China from 1979 to 2016 led to more abortion based on sex, and the killing and abandonment of small girls in that country. There were various exemptions from the policy for ethnic minorities and families whose first child was a girl (clear evidence in itself of the cultural preference for sons). Further, the assertion of the link with pre-selection and infanticide has sometimes been disputed in this vast and still too secretive part of the world. Some, for example, point to a likely under-reporting of baby girls in families which breached the one-child rule as an explanation for the disparity in numbers. However, in 2011 in the *British Medical Bulletin*, J. Nie suggested there were up to 40 million missing women as a result of the less palatable explanation.

This dramatic preference for boys is far from limited to Asia, and the Council of Europe Commissioner for Human Rights has long raised concerns about 'skewed sex ratios at birth' (levels above 110 and up to 116 newborn boys to every 100 girls), attributable to sex-selective abortions in Albania, Armenia, Azerbaijan, Georgia, Montenegro, Kosovo and parts of the Former Yugoslav Republic of Macedonia.

The preference also expresses itself strongly in countries where sex-selective abortion is less prevalent, or acceptable or documented. A 2011 Gallup poll in the USA asked participants what their sex preference would be if they were allowed to have only one child; 40 per cent of respondents favoured a boy compared with only 28 per cent preferring a daughter. The poll also highlighted a lack of ethical consensus around gender-based pre-selection, with another 40 per cent of American respondents believing that choosing embryos by sex is an acceptable part of reproductive rights and autonomy. Selection on this basis was offered in about half of US fertility clinics in 2006 and even on non-medical grounds. If, among the wealthy at least, fertility is thought of more and more as a right and not a privilege and IVF increasingly becomes a matter of profit for the service provider and of choice rather than necessity for the consumer, one can imagine selection on the basis of a whole host of non-life-damaging or threatening characteristics – including sex – becoming normalized.

Despite attempts at outlawing parental pre-birth sex selection at international, regional and national legislative levels (sex-selective abortion was made illegal in China in 2005), some activists argue that the practice should not be criminalized or even discouraged in certain contexts. Some of them understandably fear the outcomes and motives of any incursion into a woman's right to an abortion, even when she chooses it on the basis of the sex of the unborn. They cite public education campaigns in some countries that focus on moral evils of abortion per se rather than the valuing of girls. They point to the mental health and other risks to both mother and baby, if the former should ever feel compelled to carry an unwanted unborn child, whatever the reasons for those feelings. Others point to societies where a woman who repeatedly produces girls but not boys will face ill-treatment and even be made an outcast. The logic continues that to succeed in prohibiting pre-selective abortion in some societies would lead only to a related increase in infanticide. The arguments, however evidence-based and context-specific, make for depressing reading and are a brutal indictment on the social, economic and cultural lot of girls and women in too many places.

So my hypothetical question to you appears to remain all too real for a great many parents and would-be parents all over our modern world who have both practical reasons and deep-seated prejudices for preferring sons to daughters. Further, it would seem that these reasons do not automatically dissipate with greater literacy, wealth or so-called economic progress alone. And yet those daughters will still come. What determines sex and gender? What is it to be a girl and a woman thereafter? And who decides?

For the avoidance of doubt and without spending too much time on exploring the ambiguities and fluidities of definition (this being an attempt at practical political progress rather than philosophical perfection), I use 'sex' first as

6

based on bodies and second as recognized by law. 'Gender' refers to the ornate social and cultural constructs built upon the foundations of differences of sex.

It is all too easy – at least with sex – to point to the xx and xy chromosomes and subsequent hormones that determine female and male from the moment of conception. Yet that is just the beginning of the conversation biologically, let alone culturally, socially, politically and economically. Rare chromosomal conditions and variations in hormone production can lead to a whole range of degrees on the feminine to masculine physical spectrum. Further, the relationship between biology and learning respectively on psychology and behaviour remain constantly and highly contested. Cordelia Fine's 2017 *Testosterone Rex* is a brilliantly lucid and ultimately optimistic exposition of the science relating to the complex cocktail of biology and environment that shapes sex and gender. In it she debunks so many myths relating to our supposedly fixed male and female natures that you want to thrust the book into the hands of every reactionary or complacent parent, policy-maker, commentator, consumer and boss as an urgent invitation to think again.

And yet inequality between the sexes is so entrenched that policing, or escaping or redefining the border is for many a life's work and struggle. We see such contests always and everywhere from debates about characteristic or even appropriate masculine and feminine traits, behaviours and identities, and more recently in those involving trans men and women. As with other badges of identity and other forms of divide and rule, the categories would not matter so much if so much did not turn on them. If we weren't all in prison, there would be no need to assign us to a male, female or unisex institution.

Unsurprisingly perhaps and for the longest time, debates

around sex and gender revolved around and were preoccupied with reproduction. Sexual difference is after all primarily defined by the difference in sexual organs. So the need or desire to procreate combined with hierarchical social and economic systems to define women all over the world primarily by reference to the capacity for and function of childbirth and child rearing. Once upon a time many feminists thought that the advent of accessible and effective contraception, reproductive choice, medical advances and more general sexual autonomy would change all that and liberate women. Yet for a host of reasons, this has not come to pass.

Firstly, there are still too many women in the world denied basic bodily integrity, let alone reproductive control by their families, communities, traditions and laws.

Secondly, even in the societies where a greater range of female aspirations is legally and theoretically possible, women's more diverse ambitions are not always matched with an equal generosity of expectation, judgement and provision by others (whether men, women or society). The childless woman of child-bearing or post-child-bearing age is too often expected to explain her situation in a way that the highly educated woman who never works or who gives up even prestigious and well-paid work on having children is not. Too often and for too many, the easiest or even socially 'correct' explanation is to sigh wistfully or allude to not having been 'blessed'. This is in no way to detract from the many deliberate, happy and fulfilled mothers, but merely to point out and recognize a world of loaded expectation and judgement which also lacks childcare support for working women.

Thirdly and even when reproduction is taken out of the equation or immediate expectation, societal and male ideals about femininity do not necessarily progress. The internet now provides greater access and exposure to endless advertising and pornography that reinforce the objectification of women as passive sex toys to be used, abused and cast aside – including by way of violence.

Fourthly, many describe a global crisis in masculinity (the flip-side of this divide and rule) caused by and in reaction to post-industrialized economies, or greater female education and aspiration, or a clash of traditions or all of the above. If you were brought up to believe that a 'real man' is a strong, brave or even competitive and aggressive breadwinner outside the home (even in class and social contexts where women have always been or often had to be breadwinners too), how do you adjust to being out of work or out of a sufficiently secure, remunerative or prestigious job while 'others' – in the form of women or foreign nationals – appear to make either substantial advances or simple demands? And if, unlike many women, you as a man have not been socialized to share your emotional burden by confiding in friends, colleagues or loved ones, how much greater the risk of it exploding into profound depression, rage, violence or suicide?

Ultimately there is power and money to be made and retained by the fears, anxieties and divisions of most of us. If I don't like my appearance, you can sell me new clothing, diets and skin products. If I am guilty about my parenting or have no affordable childcare, I may be more likely to accept that part-time, low-paid and insecure work. If I am afraid of losing my job, I may not seek to organize with others to stand up for our shared work conditions and security. And so it goes on.

Some of the contemporary discourse around trans women provides a disappointingly familiar twist on perennial anxieties around identity. This time it isn't suffragettes being shouted at in the street for not being 'real women', or good wives or mothers but ironically some self-avowed feminists questioning the authenticity or 'realness' of trans women. The tone, volume and levels of courtesy of these debates vary hugely on both sides (especially on social media), but they seem to contain some recurring refrains.

In dealing with this question, I am making a conscious decision not to quote individual commentators or particular media storms at this point. Some of the rows have brought more heat than light to the debate, igniting controversy rather than advancing understanding. Instead I will refer to two hypothetical advocates and attempt to paraphrase the competing arguments as I understand them.

Jane is a feminist writer and activist with many years of achievements and accolades under her belt. She is clear that she in no way means to be transphobic and supports the rights of people to transition to whatever body and lifestyle might make them happy. However, she thinks that trans women ought not to consider or describe themselves as 'real' women for the following reasons.

Firstly, she argues that trans women are not sufficiently biologically female to be in the same category as Jane and others like her. Secondly, while they have suffered their own struggles and oppressions, to have been born and lived as a male is by definition to have enjoyed a life of privilege up until transition. This, Jane says, makes the lived experience of trans and 'cis' women (whose gender identity matches their birth sex) obviously different. Thus, when trans women enter Jane's women's rooms, spaces and platforms, they somehow take them away from other women who still need them. Thirdly, being a woman and a feminist is so interconnected with the experience of menstruation and reproduction and the politics of reproductive rights that a woman without these concerns does not readily fit into the same struggle. Fourthly, she thinks that too many trans women undermine feminist struggles with ambitions to attain and portray a hyper-feminine cliché that is categorized by long legs, hair, make-up, high heels and even publicly confessing to enjoying the experience of receiving wolf whistles, etc. Thus the ideals and aspirations of too many trans women seem to Jane to run directly counter to her view of the interests and causes of women like her. Fifthly, she points to a number of circumstances where to put vulnerable women such as rape survivors in a women's refuge or prison in close quarters with a pre- or non-operative trans woman would be to put them at risk, or if not actually at risk, at least in profound anxiety. Finally, she worries that to transition via hormones and surgery, particularly at a relatively young age, might be an attempt to conform to societal pressures and stereotypes around sex and sexuality rather than to escape them. And regret might well follow later in life.

JN is a young trans person, writer and activist. They had a very difficult childhood and adolescence as a boy experiencing bullying, abuse and violence and the mental health issues and suicidal thoughts that came as a consequence of that ordeal. JN is saddened by Jane's position and indeed by that of some other activists who argue that broad and inclusive LGBT umbrellas are no longer sustainable because the lives and struggles of lesbian, gay and bisexual cis people are too different from the trans experience. They respond to Jane as follows.

Firstly, they challenge Jane's biological binary as clumsy and even artificial in relation to hormonal differences, intersex classifications and so on. Secondly, they remind Jane that even cis women have had so many different lived experiences based on class, race, place and generation that JN might actually have a great deal more in common with some cis women (e.g. refugees), who have experienced extreme poverty and violence – including sexual violence – than Jane with the greater safety that has come with her own privilege. Thirdly, they ask, wasn't feminism supposed to be about freeing women from the obligation as opposed to the choice to reproduce? So why would Jane exclude anyone from the sisterhood on the grounds of being unable to conceive, gestate and give birth? JN also reminds Jane of the many cis women who do not reproduce through choice, inability or circumstance. Indeed Jane herself is a significantly older woman and it seems strange to JN that, even at this stage in life, she should continue to choose to make reproduction such an important marker of identity. Fourthly, JN points out that there are a great many cis women who prop up and positively relish all the clichés of women's ideal appearance and behaviour that hold them back. Indeed there are many cis women who detest the notion of feminism, who make excuses for inequality and chauvinism. Some even subject their own daughters to FGM. Are they any less entitled to call themselves women for being wrong? Then, JN is uncomfortable with what they perceive as Jane's apparent implication that anyone with a penis inherently constitutes a predatory threat to women. While JN doesn't lay this at Jane's door, JN has been angered and upset by public rows in the US and elsewhere about which public bathrooms trans people should be allowed to use. These are reminiscent of racial segregation in apartheid South Africa and the pre-civil rights USA. As for women's refuges and prisons, there are surely many people who should not be housed or imprisoned together for a number of different incompatibilities of history or behaviour. Prison and other authorities with a duty of care to their charges must make decisions about the placement of violent or mentally vulnerable or suicidal people all the time. Surely, if no one size fits all in all of these circumstances, why should one size or shape be used to exclude self-identifying trans women who are hurting no one and only trying to cope in a far from perfect world like everyone else?

My instinct, as you might predict, is to come to this debate with a best attempt at a human rights perspective. If we are all human first and foremost, our cause as seekers of justice and equality is surely not to compete with any among us for victimhood, or biological or social purity. I appreciate that this begs the question as to who is truly 'among us', but as the daughter of migrants to the only 'home country' I have ever known, my default can hardly be to scrutinize or rail against anyone's greater or lesser 'realness' or right to self-define. It is so hard to be a woman. It is to be in the secondary rather than the primarily understood notion of personhood. In the eyes of too many, it is to be something other and less than a man. Why should I exclude or deport any migrant or refugee to my sex or gender, particularly if they come in peace and armed with an understanding of the multiple identities and barriers that black or poor or abused or strong or political women face? So I think that I am more with JN than Jane in the argument between them. But surely neither should be reviled and shut down as long as the debate is conducted in a spirit of mutual respect rather than one of vilification and abuse.

The central and circular problem is that all being 'human first and foremost' may be the ideal but it is certainly not the lived reality anywhere in the world. Women have been variously, poignantly and accurately described as 'the second sex' (Simone de Beauvoir), or in a category of slavery or 'perpetual childhood' or somewhere between men and beasts (Mary Wollstonecraft). This being the case, some feminists might see a trans person who migrates from either side of the gender or sex border (often with great personal and financial cost, effort and anguish) as somehow reinforcing it. Yet surely a trans person's journey might just as easily be viewed as highlighting a more fluid, flexible or illogical border, whose oppressions and injustices we might aspire to erase to the point when the category of 'human' finally becomes the most inclusive, empowering and real?

The comparison of sex, gender and race is far from perfect; sex being a social and political exaggeration of biology and gender and race closer to pure fiction. Analogy between even sex and race can, it seems to me, be occasionally instructive nonetheless. Whatever people's private opinions, I have noticed far less public controversy and outcry (especially among feminists and other progressives) when people identified as female at birth transition to become trans men. Perhaps it is thought more understandable or even sympathetic to seek to escape a more down-trodden category of humanity for a more privileged or apparently liberated one.

Similarly, whatever some people's feelings about the anglicization of 'foreign-sounding' names, or hair-straightening, skin-lightening and so on, I have rarely – at least in recent times – known such an outpouring of righteous race-based indignation as that directed at the American activist Rachel Dolezal. Born to 'white' parents of Czech, German and Swedish descent, Dolezal (who changed her name to Nkechi Amare Diallo) describes herself as having strongly associated with the identity and oppression of Black Americans in a highly racialized society. She taught African-American history, became president of her local NAACP (National Association for the Advancement of Colored People), braided her hair and presented as 'black' before being effectively outed, mocked and ostracized by many in both white and black America for 'cultural appropriation and fraud'. What she sees as personal discovery, self-identity and political solidarity, others see as some form of strange, illogical and subversive treachery. This is a charge often laid against those who fail to conform with accepted norms relating to sex, gender, sexuality and even class. And to be deliberately 'downwardly mobile' is perhaps to be the most threatening of all, for to give up your privileged status might be to undermine a worldview based on inequality.

Do you remember when you first had any real sense of being male or female? How did this happen and what did it seem to mean? I was born in 1969 and thus experienced early childhood in a decade of apparent social progress, at least in the UK and in the relations between women and men. Nonetheless, I was dressed on special occasions in classic cartoon-like frilled dresses, assigned pink birthday cakes and decorations and bought dolls. In fairness, I also had jeans and trainers in which I rode my bicycle and kicked a football against a wall. Crucially I was taught to read before I started primary school. Watching the boys around me highlighted the difference. Their clothes and birthday cakes were blue and their toys were cars, swords and guns. The weapons I coveted and borrowed, the cars not so much. But who could resist running around as the cowboys or soldiers of stories, films and television rather than passively rocking a plastic blonde baby girl – even one that amazingly shed tears?

My mother was an interesting role model in this respect. She was at the same time the culprit who taught me to read, the demure feminine beauty I would never live up to and the self-avowed former 'tomboy' who had climbed trees in her own childhood and who would occasionally momentarily escape the drudgery and limitations of her thirties by playing tag or scary monsters with her then small child. Like so many other children, I was raised inside a contradiction of theory and practice. Both my parents nurtured my desire for learning, striving and argument, and there was never a thought that I wouldn't study and work. Yet my own university-educated mother had fled a chauvinist father in India to come to London and ultimately became a home-maker. Conversely, my father was for many years the sole family breadwinner, commuting four hours a day to and from his work as a book-keeper – work that today might be done at least partly remotely, and by fewer people. He barely saw his family during the week and his wife no doubt spent many a lonely day with only her small child for company, at least until she began to work part-time as a shop assistant when I was ten years old. I never envied or aspired to either of their lives.

Sex and gender distinction became more and more real at school. The physical space of the playground was seemingly eternally dominated by that permanent game of football engaging most of the boys while the girls were consigned to the margins to chat, skip or play games of imaginative role play.

Forty-odd years later, the gendering of childhood seems to have changed relatively little, and some even suggest that in many respects the stereotyping of toys and clothes may have now become even worse. The most cursory of internet searches will still produce rival offerings in pink and blue, even when the items themselves (such as cameras and trainers) appear not to be particularly gendered in the adult world. Why do we do it? Why does it matter?

A person's sex identity is probably the first thing that you notice and the last thing you forget about them. At least I know this is true of my own imperfect mind. When pregnant many years ago, I developed the habit of talking to my unborn cargo each morning during a twenty-or-so-minute walk to work. I think I had read somewhere or other that this was a good thing to do, but in truth I suspect I was trying to get used to the terrifying prospect of motherhood. I was absolutely clear in my own mind that I had no preference at all as to the baby's sex. Yet I was also clear that when the opportunity to find out arose at the relevant scan, I wanted to have the information. I told myself that it was simply a question of medical and personal autonomy. I believed that those parents who deliberately refused to be told on the grounds that they 'wanted the surprise', were ridiculously romantic, old-fashioned and perhaps even superstitious. There was no way that the men and women in white coats should know anything about my 'condition' without also sharing it with me. However, I also recall that once I knew that my baby was a boy, the conversations on my walk to work qualitatively and dramatically changed. Don't get me wrong. I didn't start talking about football, fighter planes or investment banking and never really have. This confession is of nothing quite so crass. What changed was my new ability to imagine the abstract baby as a real one and therefore to connect emotionally. I was now motivated by something that felt a bit less like a carrier's duty and a bit more like human love. At least that is what I think happened.

The revelation that 'it's a boy' or 'it's a girl' is routinely the primary birth announcement that precedes even news of the state of the health of mother and newborn. It may well be intended by many (and at least initially) as simply a means of giving some first form of human identity and personality to an infant. After all, the newborn is yet to have many discernible talents and opinions to feed the imagination of eager friends and family. Yet even this simple and apparently innocent message comes with strings. These quickly become ties and then chains as we exaggerate and fortify the differences between these unequal categories of humanity. Wittingly or unwittingly, we teach our boys and girls to fit in and know their preordained place rather than to choose, build, take or share it. So each real or virtual aisle of pink or blue products for babies, toddlers and even older children might as well be a neon-lit conveyor belt to our segregated prisons.

As far as I can tell from both the available scientific research and cultural history, there is nothing intrinsically feminine or masculine about pink and blue respectively. This is evidenced by the relatively recent predominantly American and Western European adoption of these codes – some say as late as the 1940s and not entrenching until some time later. Indeed many commentators suggest that as late as 1918, some US catalogues were favouring exactly the opposite uniform with pink (allegedly the stronger colour) as more appropriate for boys and (the dainty) blue as a natural girls' colour. Earlier traditions and those elsewhere in the world favour more gender-neutral and often white clothing for infants for several years into their young lives; no doubt for reasons of convenience in relation to the making, laundering and recycling of clothes between a number of children in both the immediate family and well beyond.

Experiments in which babies and toddlers are asked to express a preference between the now stereotypical Western feminine and masculine colours show no real preference in the earliest months but move towards a significant preference for the 'normal' colour as toddlers become aware of society's expectations around gender. At just this stage, my own son seemed to be aware of the social significance of pink before he could even name the colour. He attended co-educational daycare from the age of six months, and I shall never forget my amusement when, at around the age of two, he named colours that I pointed to as red, 'lello', blue, green and 'Barbie'. Later on in adult life, contemporary surveys suggest that blue is a favourite and pink a relatively unpopular colour among both sexes internationally. What does any of this demonstrate? That compulsory difference sells and that late twentieth-century and early twenty-first-century consumerism feeds off it. If all infants wore laundry-friendly white, or planet-friendly off-white or even a rash of bold washable coloured clothes that could be recycled within a family and community regardless of the sex of the children, someone would make less money selling us stereotypes and land-fill.

I have heard the counter-claim of many a feminist mother (including one with boy and girl twins) that they were absolutely religious in their attempts to bestow cars on their daughters and dolls on their sons, only to watch the gender-oppositional toys swapped or discarded. I cannot help but find such arguments inflated in their notion of maternal power, or at least a little naive as to the role of other overwhelming cultural influences on small children from both inside and outside the home.

If you think I go too far, try another thought experiment. How would you feel about such active and constant consumer suggestion along the lines of any other characteristic of identity, however fixed or fluid? How about explicitly marketing plastic manual tools in the poorer parts of town and first computers and chemistry sets only to the children in more affluent neighbourhoods?

And what about race? We have rightly long abandoned the offensive 'golliwog' soft toy of a bygone imperial age and it is finally possible to buy a black Barbie doll. If we can understand the importance of such changes in the context of how young children of all races see themselves in relation to others, why can we not see the value of abandoning the pink and blue (or at least the pink) and actively offering both dolls and Lego to the future parents of future boys and girls?

I appreciate how easy it is to trivialize the argument that even small, subtle and repeated differences in the treatment of people, especially when they are young and at their most malleable, make a long-term difference. But I believe they do. That is why discrimination is and has always been such a pernicious and degrading influence in the world. It may seem trivial to the disinterested observer but not to the person forced to sit at the back of the bus or the person who is groped on it. It may be irrelevant to the person never, let alone repeatedly, stopped and searched or otherwise harassed, however politely, while others go about their business unimpeded. But like water on stone, even the most seemingly petty discrimination, segregation or injustice works away at the soul to produce self-doubt, even self-loathing, resentment and a waste of life. I completely understand and positively share concerns as to the dangers of attempting to iron out all difference in the pursuit of equality. History has shown how it brings enormous risks to individuality, freedom and creativity. But equally to entrench and enforce either grossly exaggerated or completely artificial difference in the form of stereotyping girls and boys in the cause of rampant consumerism certainly brings its own form of harsh and uniformed totalitarianism.

It seems to me that if we as human beings are ever to free ourselves and each other from such damaging constraint, we have surely to start at the very beginning. We must begin by freeing our minds. In his 1990 essay ' "But would that still be me?" Notes on gender, "race", ethnicity as sources of "identity" ', world-renowned philosophy professor Kwame Anthony Appiah resolves the question like this:

In a truly nonsexist, nonracist society, gender, the ethical identity constructed on the base of sexual differences, would at least be radically differently configured, and might, like 'race' entirely wither away . . .

Once again, however, the proposition is to some extent circular. The ethical identity difference of gender might well wither in the 'truly nonsexist . . . society', but how can we possibly hope to build this place without first dismantling at least some of the entrenched distinctions and assumptions conceptually? You might call it yet another obvious case of which came first – the woman or the egg?

Judith Butler is another internationally celebrated American philosophy professor who displays considerable comfort and dexterity with notions of complex and multiple identity. In her now legendary *Gender Trouble: Feminism and the Subversion of Identity*, she offers the following helpful insights:

Perhaps paradoxically 'representation' will be shown to make sense for feminism only when the subject of 'women' is nowhere presumed.

Perhaps a coalition needs to acknowledge its contradictions and take action with those contradictions intact.

So perhaps my circular problem requires a paradoxical response. While I see discrimination and oppression on the grounds of sex and gender as being the most prevalent human rights violation in the world, the collateral damage or victimhood is in fact suffered by those on both sides of the deliberately exaggerated divide (women and men), as well as those who either choose to be or find themselves in 'no man's land' (people who don't predominantly identify in these binary categories or who find themselves wrongly defined by their bodies, law or society). We cannot even aspire to a less gendered and unequal society if we cannot begin to give both sex and gender less prominence and a more equal consideration alongside other aspects of humanity and personality in our own imaginations. Perhaps ironically, the online world that has provided an all too safe space for misogyny might nonetheless – with its anonymity and avatars – provide opportunities for gender-neutral imagination and conversation.

To quote Butler once more:

If one 'is' a woman, that is surely not all one is . . .

This kind of thinking may of course present challenges when adopting some positive interventions such as affirmative political, legislative and economic action in the cause of attempting to activate and speed up the progress of equality. Yet it seems to me that any such difficulties may be temporary, marginal, soluble and ultimately worthwhile. For to be too harshly exclusive in defining and policing the oldest oppressed category of 'woman' is ironically to make both the sex and gender divide even harder to dismantle or dissolve. To jealously protect our particular victimhood is ultimately to make harder our escape. If the house is too secure from that feared intrusion, we become our own jailers and risk being trapped in a fire.

So to return to my original question as to which sex you would choose for yourself or your only child, the goal must surely be that even as choosing becomes more scientifically viable, its significance or desirability becomes increasingly politically obsolete.

2. Misrepresentation

It was excruciating. The forty-fifth president of the United States grabbed and patted the hand of Britain's second woman prime minister and she allowed him to do it. What hope for the political obsolescence of sexual difference when the leaders of two of the oldest democracies parade themselves in such a pantomime? The politics of the extraordinary image will haunt Theresa May and no doubt other women in leadership for a very long time. As she appeared to crawl before Donald Trump, the skins of millions of proud women around the world crawled too. The clean-up operation went into a rapid spin cycle with briefings about the president's alleged infirmity when walking on gradients. But the 'slope not grope' theory didn't account for the repeated hand-holding or the fact that the former *Apprentice* TV star had not been filmed or spotted seeking equivalent manual support from any males of the species. It was a sad day for our sex. Mrs May is a Conservative and I am of the left, but before her 'hand-gate' incident, I had always rather admired her seemingly feminist instincts. Kind and encouraging to other women, at least with her type of politics, the prime minister had always traded on being feminine without being flirtatious and more than capable of repelling misogyny of whatever type and from whatever source. Of course this was months before she presided over one of the nastiest general election campaigns in modern British history and allowed our most senior black woman politician to become the target of personal derision. Mercifully that election campaign proved to be as foolhardy as it was unpleasant.

The previous year, during her short Conservative leadership campaign that became a coronation, Theresa May's supporters rightly rounded on ill-judged remarks by an ill-fated female rival suggesting that May's lack of children somehow made her a less qualified candidate for the highest office. When she first visited that other UK female leader, Scotland's First Minister Nicola Sturgeon, both senior politicians had to fight to get the great British media to pay more attention to their discussions than their legs. And years earlier as Conservative Party chair, May famously popularized the phrase 'Nasty Party' as a description of her own political movement with its unreconstructed social attitudes. But her first White House visit was a low. This is easy to say in prose and hindsight. So what do I think she could or should have done?

First there is the narrow and immediate question of what to do with the president's hand. Sadly every adult woman on the planet – and probably all too many a girl – has had to learn how to handle inappropriate male touching in a number of contexts. Granted, the gaze of the world's media and a Brexit-inspired desperation to make a trade deal no doubt added considerable pressure to an awkward social moment. But instinct and experience should have come together to prevent the extended embarrassment of the president holding and patting the prime minister's hand and the lasting images of the man robbing the woman of all power and dignity, let alone equality, in such an exposed situation. I am assuming that the gesture was not agreed or choreographed in advance. That possibility is far too distasteful even to imagine. So let's assume that the hand grab was an unscripted and unilateral gesture on the part of Mrs May's host. What if she had held the hand firm for just a second, then shaken it and removed her own to pat the president on the back? Isn't a pat on the back rather than hand-holding the contemporary traditional way that male leaders demonstrate amity and power-play simultaneously? Haven't we watched endless news footage of great men at summits? Each insists that the other goes through the door first so as to receive the friendly and only slightly patronizing (depending on those involved) back pat?

Then there is the considerable underlying problem of too eager and close a public association between the woman who had been so keen to self-identify as a Church of England vicar's daughter and the less than completely wholesome President Trump. He is an overt, shameless and perhaps even proud misogynist. Not just a little insensitive or unreconstructed or chauvinistic. His repeated and publicly expressed attitudes to women in general, as well as those he sees as intimates, desired intimates and opponents in particular, are notoriously hateful and almost unprintable. He has openly called women 'dogs', 'bitches' and 'pieces of ass' and bragged about getting away with indecent touching and grabbing of them on account of his wealth and power. In a 'hot mike' accidental recording from 2005 the man who would be president talks of his entitlement to 'grab' women 'by the pussy'. He once demeaned a challenging woman journalist by allusion to menstruation, and has even joked about incest, making public comments about his daughter that would be considered taboo in most societies around the world. He has frequently defined, praised and undermined women by reference to his view of their physical appearance and ridiculed his former presidential rival the former Secretary of State Hillary Clinton on Twitter, for failing to 'satisfy' her husband – the forty-second US president.

One of Trump's first presidential acts and now infamous Executive Orders reinstated the anti-abortion 'global gagging order' first introduced by Ronald Reagan in 1984. This bans US financial aid to organizations providing abortions or abortion advice around the world. Yet another piece of unforgettable Trump iconography is the photograph of him signing the order flanked by half a dozen men in dark suits without a woman anywhere in sight. To be fair and as with his positions on torture, Muslims and Mexico, he had flagged, even telegraphed on the campaign trail that there would have to be 'some form of punishment' for women under a new regime where the US banned abortion. He was prepared and even eager to bury his pro-choice attitudes of the 1990s so as to placate the socially conservative Republican base, but not, it seems, his lifetime of so-called 'locker room talk' about women. A witty and silent repost to Trump and his men in grey suits may be found in a subsequent image of Sweden's Deputy Prime Minister Isabella Lovin. Surrounded by seven women colleagues, one heavily pregnant, she is pictured signing a new progressive climate law.

Mrs May's dash to the White House is also worth comparing with the more cautious approach of the more experienced German Chancellor Angela Merkel. Another European leader of the right of centre, Merkel welcomed refugees to her country in marked contrast with May's attitude to human rights issues and attracted some criticism from Trump when he was but a presidential pretender. Merkel famously congratulated him on his election in a letter that was more than courteous and yet still strong, values-driven and even interpreted by many as a word of gentle warning:

Germany and America are bound by common values – democracy, freedom, as well as respect for the rule of law and the dignity of each and every person, regardless of their origin, skin colour, creed, gender, sexual orientation, or political views. It is based on these values that I wish to offer close cooperation, both with me personally and between our countries' governments.

Then, following another presidential order comprising a blanket ban on nationals from a number of predominantly Muslim countries (where Trump had no business links) from entering the US, Merkel was said to have 'explained' the Refugee Convention to the rookie world leader over the telephone. And soon after May's White House visit and while 1.8 million Britons lent their names to a petition protesting against Trump's planned state visit to the United Kingdom, Merkel was seen instead welcoming the young Liberal and self-proclaimed feminist Canadian Premier Justin Trudeau for talks in Berlin. Predictably (and perhaps still smarting from the May–Trump images), a British media outlet described her as looking at Trudeau 'with doe eyes' in a photograph of a dinner where she was clearly in command of an encounter that more resembled a positive but professional board meeting.

President Trump's election represents a significant setback for women and girls the world over. What signals do his comments and actions send to men and boys about the acceptability of treating women as little more than chattels or livestock? What signals to girls and women about how they should see themselves and their lot? My critics and Trump's fans and apologists counter with comparisons with the Middle East and other parts of the world where women are demeaned, objectified and even owned. But this is an obviously specious argument. Old unbroken democracies like the UK and US are supposed to be better than that.

Individual American states began granting women the right to vote from the late 1890s (well before any women could vote in the UK) and the 19th amendment to the US Constitution granted full voting rights in 1920. The significance of the new Trump symbolism is made even worse when you consider that he came as a political outsider to beat (however narrowly) a woman favourite and the first serious female candidate for the American presidency in its history.

There is no doubt a host of reasons for what Theresa May called Trump's 'stunning election victory'. The populist right has benefited globally from the financial crisis of 2008 when political, banking and business elites were seen to suffer the least or not at all from a disaster of their own making and from which so many poor and middle-income people have suffered the most. Mrs Clinton was perhaps seen by many to be too much part of that failed establishment. Her experience and relationship to wealth and political continuity may ironically have smoothed her path to the Democratic nomination only to cost her the presidency itself. A further irony lies in the billionaire playboy tycoon Trump presenting himself as the rebel outsider on the side of ordinary people. That extraordinary con was compounded by xenophobia and racism and facilitated by an aspirational but disposable reality TV culture. The power of old-style misogyny and new social media became a very toxic and potent cocktail indeed.

What Mrs May found 'stunning' others found 'shocking', but the victory of President Trump may be explicable nonetheless. Divide and rule is an age-old tactic for gaining and keeping power from those who have never known it or who lose or surrender it. The biggest surprise is that disdain and even hatred of women should be as marketable or excusable as Islamophobia or xenophobia in the USA in 2017, and even among such a sizeable number of women themselves. While there are very few women, even on the far right of American politics, who would actively defend Trump's worst remarks, many would excuse them and even more would put up with them, in consideration of other concerns that they find greater and identifications which they feel more strongly.

The numbers are worth considering. Polls suggest that as many as 53 per cent of white American women voted for the Republican nominee. Among white women without a college degree the ratio for and against Trump rises to nearly two to one. Conversely, among white women with degrees, Clinton obtained only 51 per cent support as against Trump's 45 per cent. By contrast, BAME women voted overwhelmingly for Clinton with 94 per cent of black women and 68 per cent of Latino women supporting the Democratic nominee. Perhaps race is a more entrenched badge of identity than sex or gender in the United States? Or perhaps women have heard so much Trump talk in their family, social and work lives that it now fails to shock, even when uttered by someone seeking the highest office in the land?

> What are you gonna do? Lock us all up? We're in every home, we're half the human race, you can't stop us all.

These are the words of Maud Watts (played by Carey Mulligan) in Sarah Gavron and Abi Morgan's great 2015 film *Suffragette*. The fact of women's numbers and ubiquity gives inspiration and hope in that story and in life. But as struggles for other forms of justice have continually demonstrated, numbers only deliver strength with an element of solidarity and being in 'every home' means that other loyalties – especially those of family and history – will always provide an alternative pull.

Female solidarity may not have kept Donald Trump out of the White House but it has certainly inspired a strong protest response to his election in America and all over the world. The US marches were said to be the largest and most peaceful in the country's history, and when the turnout was combined with those who marched in the UK and elsewhere, it became one of the largest mass demonstrations in world history – beaten only narrowly by those that followed the Charlie Hebdo atrocity in Paris two years earlier and, significantly, by those against the Iraq War in 2003.

The London gathering (of around 100,000) was a uniquely inspiring affair. Mothers and daughters, work colleagues and friends of different generations marched against Trump primarily for his misogyny, but there were many placards about his stances on refugees and wall-building too. There were many expat American women of all ages as well as people who seemed wholly unused to spending their Saturdays this way. The Mayfair pub that one strand used as an assembly point was a picture. A handful of regulars (mostly young men) had come to watch the football and have lunch. They soon found themselves engulfed by women pre-protesters but mostly took the invasion in good part, drank their beer, studied their burger menus and took advice from the bar staff on when things were likely to calm down. Ironically it was one female football fan out with her male partner who seemed the most annoyed, and for a moment I was reminded of being a young school child on public transport causing irritation to 'members of the public' by being part of too large and uniformed a cohort. But the moment was glorious nonetheless and I will never forget the woman of a certain age who came to seek out those I assumed to be her work colleagues. She sat at our table in the fairly nondescript heaving bar, armed with a large glass of white wine. 'I've never been on a march before . . .' she told me. 'I nearly came out over Iraq but my children were small and I . . .' I smiled and nodded. Her colleagues found her. They seemed so glad that she had joined them that day.

This mostly – but by no means exclusively – female demonstration was marked by its good humour and sense of the same. Some marchers dressed as suffragettes carried placards with slogans about different clothes but the same struggles. Others went for the jugular with 'Free Melania' (a reference to the new first lady) and 'We shall comb-over' (a reference to the president's legendary hair). Trade unionists marched alongside students and stay-at-home mothers and Queen's Counsel. That such a diverse and yet collective event could be pulled together so quickly is no doubt a credit to the internet. And yet, like the printing press before it, that phenomenal innovation has its light and dark side when it comes to social progress.

The role and use of Twitter and other forms of social media are worth examining in relation to the lot of women in general and the rise of Trump in particular. The internet is perhaps the greatest technological innovation of my lifetime. It is a perfect example of an advancement that causes history to accelerate out of kilter with its previous rhythm, like entering 'warp speed' in the sci-fi TV shows of the late 1960s. Like the printing press, it has in so many ways been a huge force for freedom, equality and democracy, giving vital information and voice to so many previously isolated and unheard people. Human rights abuses and the revolutions they inspired have been transmitted around the world in seconds, bypassing state- and oligarch-controlled conventional media. Impoverished campaigners have been able to access important research data without the archives and staff available to corporates and governments. And these campaigners have included a new generation of feminists all over the world.

The Everyday Sexism Project was started by the formidable Laura Bates in the UK. It now gives women a platform to chart and discuss every form of discrimination, indignity and abuse internationally. The not-for-profit Women's Media Center 'Women Under Siege' programme has harnessed the unique capabilities of the internet to map and document the numerous incidences of sexual assault that suggest that rape is being used systematically as a weapon of war by the government and government-aligned forces in Syria. And there are numerous other fine examples of everyone from activists, journalists, politicians, musicians and actors using their experience, skills and profile to highlight the women's cause online. So the internet can clearly be a vital tool in raising awareness and even organizing against both casual and extreme sexism and misogyny on a local, national and international scale. And given the potential speed and scale of campaigning in this new world, it can even be harnessed to fight for greater responsibility and protection from those who provide and profit from individual platforms themselves.

Yet the dark side is equal and opposite and has spawned a whole new hell of misogynistic abuse often laced with racism, menaces and direct intimidation. It goes well beyond the grey and disputed borderline of hate speech and deep into the land of threats to rape, maim and kill. It seems an irony to me now that, when I was young, typing seemed a predominantly female accomplishment; 1950s cinema depictions of the 'typing pool' featured well-turned-out young women gently tapping away hundreds of words a minute to a jolly rhythm punctuated by the satisfying ring of the end of a line of correspondence. In my mind at least, this image is now replaced with that of armies of online woman-haters bashing away at their computers in the dark, punching the keyboard as if punching their female targets; and the more high profile or political a woman – the stronger a spokesperson or role model for her sex – the greater a target she is for this new brand of pure bile.

Why should this be so? Why do some people feel so much more free to hate, insult and threaten on social media than in person, via traditional post or even by email? Is it the speed of the medium that shortens the distance and blurs the distinction between the thought and its communication? Is it online anonymity that makes the difference? Is it something about the brevity of the form or the blizzard of other users that encourages the bluntest, most shocking and sometimes cruellest expression rather than anything more reasoned, courteous or nuanced? Or is it that Twitter, in particular, turns communication into broadcasting or even into a constant online riot that is as exhilarating to some men as an old-style bar-room brawl? The 2000 film *What Women Want* featured an advertising executive played by Mel Gibson. After a domestic accident he develops the superpower of being able to hear women's thoughts without them knowing. Has the online universe become the sexual reverse of this fantasy, where women experience male hate that would previously have gone unsaid, or at least unsaid in public or decent company? Is it the medium merely exposing what was always locked away, or is there something about its design or operation that actively inspires the hatred of women? What is it about these new apparently democratic spaces that so readily lends them to the lynch mob?

Feminist campaigner Caroline Criado-Perez wrote about her own experience and that of others well before the rise of Donald Trump seemed to give even greater licence to the haters than they felt before. In her 2015 book *Do It Like a Woman* she details the abuse in stark and unsentimental terms. She remarks on how much of the fantasized and threatened violence seems to dwell on women's mouths and throats (and therefore silence) alongside sex and death (in the most brutally explicit and barbaric terms). What had Criado-Perez done to provoke such an outpouring of bile? She joined an ultimately victorious popular campaign to persuade the Bank of England that great historical women as well as men should be featured on bank notes. She was guilty of the double sin of becoming visible herself in the cause of making other women more visible and empowered.

My friend Diane Abbott is a senior UK politician and another case in point. She entered the House of Commons as Britain's first black woman Member of Parliament in 1987 and has never been a stranger to political, personal and media attack on account of her strong and articulate socialist, anti-racist and human rights' voice. Never comfortable residing anywhere near that sad place called victimhood, she spoke out against personal abuse only in February 2017. This was after a particularly harrowing flurry of online hatred directed against her caused by what she described as the 'perfect storm' of Brexit legislation and a Conservative Cabinet minister putting his arm around her in a House of Commons bar, only to text to another male Conservative colleague demeaning remarks (leaked later to a tabloid newspaper) about her appearance.

The newspaper response was predictable and telling, revelling in the intrigue but inevitably focusing not on the white male Conservative veteran's bad behaviour but instead on her instant expletive response. This appeared to give licence or encouragement to an online free-for-all that led to the suspension of a Conservative local councillor for tweeting an image of Abbott as an ape with lipstick. A great deal worse was to follow in the subsequent days and months leading up to the 2017 general election campaign in which an ultimately resilient Abbott became the deliberate target of orchestrated right-wing derision and abuse. A great communicator but nonetheless unaccustomed to taking to the page, rally, despatch box or microphone on her own behalf, the Shadow home secretary wrote a piece in the *Guardian* newspaper which was all the more poignant and shocking for the fact that she had remained silent for so long about the campaigns of targeted racist misogyny against her. She had received abuse concentrating on her race and appearance, likening her to various animals, and the rape and death threats that have become all too common against women in any form of public life. This she described as 'the politics of personal destruction', an amplified and publicly broadcasted version of the kind of emotional and threatened physical violence that women have been more used to experiencing in the cage of domestic abuse. It is as if the age-old reactionary attacks on equality and social progress begin to see women campaigners in general, but those of the left in particular, as the individual personification of all they are ideologically opposed to. So they become fair game for annihilation, by any means necessary or momentarily satisfying.

. . . suppose that someone had told me back then that thirty years on I would be receiving stuff like this: 'Pathetic useless fat black piece of shit Abbott. Just a piece of pig shit pond slime who should be fucking hung (if they could find a tree big enough to take the fat bitch's weight).' I think that even the young, fearless Diane Abbott might have paused for thought.

And that is surely the point: the Wild West of the internet is capable of giving a platform to the voiceless for good or ill. It empowers hate certainly as much as love and solidarity (some would argue more). And it creates a series of dilemmas relating to how to respond.

One option is to fight back, tweet for tweet in handset to handset combat in the moment. There might be some satisfaction in this. But surely there is also some danger for the victim of the abuse. Is she subjecting herself to greater mental and emotional torment and arguably even encouraging or rewarding the abuser with attention from the person in whom he has already demonstrated an altogether unhealthy interest? I know that this may be a controversial view and I am in no way suggesting that women should be chased away from the internet any more than they should be chased off the night-time streets. Criado-Perez writes movingly of being hurt and patronized by well-meaning women by whom she felt unsupported with their advice to turn off the machine and ignore the abuse. It is certainly not a policy that stands up to scrutiny when the analogy is made with the real or offline world.

I worry nonetheless about the greater potential for psychological intrusion of these new media. And they are continually accessed with a small personal device that is also the means of contacting friends and loved ones. It is carried around constantly; taken to the dinner table and even the bedroom, replacing both the newspaper and the alarm clock.

Another option must be to enlist online support from other users of the platform in question. This might even out the playing field. But one can imagine that witnesses to the worst abuse might feel reluctant to become its objects themselves. This leaves the option of calling out the sheriff in the form of whatever regulation and enforcement the corporate provides, or indeed the police when the nature of the abuse crosses into the realms of criminal law.

One highly sympathetic and experienced detective inspector spoke to me of his frustrations in trying to engage law enforcement in general, and prosecutors in particular. He told me stories of tweets that seemed, to me at least, to be way beyond insult and abuse, and on the cusp of incitement to violence. He told me of taking up complaints from online witnesses armed with screen-shots of the offending tweets (lest they be taken down). Then police officers in different parts of the country (perhaps far away from both victim and witness) would knock on suspects' doors, interviewing and even arresting them. It was at this point that he felt the system seemed to break down. A file was sent to a distant prosecutor who the police officer would never be able to meet and talk to. A decision on an almost tick-box pro forma might indicate no further action or action for the low-hanging fruit of a minor 'malicious communication' offence, rather than one of threat of violence. And this with little by way of explanation with which the police officer might comfort a victim or witness that they had at least been taken seriously. It seems that cuts in public spending can be as debilitating for police morale as they are to the dignity and survival of benefits claimants on the breadline.

Further, in cases where the malicious or dangerously inciting tweet had not actually been seen by its target, he was being asked to interview her and thus cause her distress, even though her evidence was unnecessary and irrelevant to proving the offence. He was worried about such a practice turning the police into reluctant agents of abuse rather than defenders against it. His tale was reminiscent of the way that sex crime and domestic abuse used to be treated – as not that serious, or not really a criminal matter or even somehow the victim's fault.

From his own working experience, he described the typical suspect of this kind of online abuse as a white man in his middle or later years, often disgruntled with his lot in life and often from a place left behind both politically and economically by ruling elites. By contrast, a great many of the targets are apparently strong women in public life. They are predominantly, but by no means exclusively, women of the left. And the life-long professional police officer (himself a white middle-aged man) spoke as if personally upset by his experience and all the more concerned given that our meeting came only months after the brutal hate-fuelled murder of Jo Cox in June 2016.

This was the first killing of a British Member of Parliament since the Conservative Ian Gow was murdered by the Provisional IRA in 1990. Cox, an impressive 41-year-old Labour MP had represented the people of Batley and Spen in West Yorkshire for less than a year after many years working in international development. Her 52-year-old constituent Thomas Mair was convicted of her murder by stabbing, shooting and then stabbing again. Described by the police as someone 'who had never held down a job, never had a girl-friend [or] any friends', Mair was a regular user of the internet at his local library. On it he searched various far-right and homicide-related topics and is said to have singled out Cox for her pro-European and immigration views. Perhaps the internet is the new frontier for a male conservative fight-back against the developing consensus around the worth of human life – if not yet respect for all people.

If a woman were subjected on a town or village street to the kind of shouted abuse that women and high-profile women in particular constantly receive online, there is little doubt that it would be taken far more seriously by existing social and legal structures. Yet, as in so many other ways, society, politics and law seem slow to catch up with and respond to the new online world. I have never been a fan of criminalizing hate speech and widely cast criminal offences such as incitement to hatred as opposed to the incitement to actual sexual or violent offences. Nor do I think that a host of extremely broad 'public order' offences should necessarily be replicated in the digital sphere. Many of these have been used and abused as a means of political control which would be especially dangerous in the present context. However, campaigns of online abuse constituting harassment, and threats to rape and kill are criminal in both the real and virtual world. If anything, there is the greater danger of their prevalence when the not so brave misogynistic bullies need not look their prey or anyone else in the eye. Police and prosecutorial authorities should be better able and equipped to deal with complaints of online criminal behaviour. I am not advocating the kind of blanket surveillance that they have sought licence for, and which does not seem to have helped the cause of women. We may be constantly watched, but we are certainly not well looked after. I am talking about the authorities having a greater understanding of this new world and its consequences, so as to be able to take specific criminal complaints seriously and then to have sufficient resources to act upon them.

If we continue with the analogy with the real world, given the corporate and monetized nature of most social media platforms, it is highly arguable that my public square or street metaphor is not the right one. Some of these social media platforms and spaces are closer in kind to a customer entering a bar, club or restaurant where the landlord is legally entitled, and perhaps even morally obliged, to regulate behaviour to a higher standard than the understandably lower threshold of the criminal law. If a man might be thrown out of McDonald's for calling a woman a pig or a bitch or a dog (without going further and actually threatening her safety), why should he not be ejected or barred from Facebook or Twitter, if such global corporate brands want to demonstrate their respect for one half of the human race? Or is it that in a world where the president of the United States is arguably an internet troll himself, the direction is towards normalizing this kind of behaviour instead of tackling it?

Even in the supposedly more genteel world of old or twentieth-century media, the representation of women beggars belief. Geena Davis is an Oscar-winning actor, perhaps most famous for her co-starring role with Susan Sarandon in the 1991 iconic two-woman road movie *Thelma and Louise*. She went on to found a research institute to engage with gender imbalance and bias in the media and entertainment industry. This in turn formulated the GD-IQ or Geena Davis Inclusion Quotient to provide automated visual analysis of the representation of women and girls in popular cinema (the top 200 grossing non-animated features). According to the Geena Davis Institute, in 2015 only 17 per cent of the top films had a female lead. Male characters received twice the amount of screen time as the female parts and this rose to three times the amount in films with a male lead. Conversely, in films with a female lead, the screen time allotted to male and female characters is roughly equal. For the same year, the institute's research suggests that male characters spoke twice as much as their female equivalents and again, this gap is even greater (three to one) in films with male leads. Yet when the cast is led by the female headliner, men and women characters speak for approximately equivalent time.

This hard data is compelling, if not so easy to explain. Is it that film-makers who cast female leads are somehow inherently more culturally progressive and so go out of their way to create equal screen and air-time between the sexes? Or is the truth more depressing, with studios feeling that the 'risk' of female-led movies requires the box-office 'ballast' of providing equivalent presence to male roles? If the answer is the latter, this research would suggest that the industry has been mistaken, as films led by women grossed an average of 15.8 per cent more than those led by men.

And it isn't just the movies that present this unbalanced view of the lives of men and women, as is demonstrated by Jennifer Siegel Newsom's 2011 award-winning documentary *Miss Representation*, which devotes the bulk of its attention to the United States, though this time covering advertising, television, film, video gaming and their relationship to the representation in positions of power and influence in that country. This time the analysis is about the often negative and even demeaning nature of the media representation, as well as its quantity. It goes on to make the argument about how we become what we see by way of testimony from teenage girls alongside some of the biggest female names in American public life. It makes for shocking but nonetheless vital viewing, and constitutes an intervention that would surely bear repeating the world over to no doubt slightly differing but nonetheless ultimately depressing results.

The triumph claimed by parts of the British press in January 2017, when the Conservative government bowed to their campaign to axe development funding to an Ethiopian project seeking to use popular media to empower women and girls, is perhaps worthy of some scrutiny. Sensationalist headlines repeatedly claimed that the Girl Effect NGO was wasting money on the creation and promotion of a girl band called Yegna ('Ours' in Amharic) and branded as the 'Ethiopian Spice Girls'. In reality the pop music was just one part of a multi-platform media campaign aimed at changing young women's attitudes towards themselves and indeed male views of them in a country where, according to UNICEF, nearly half the women have suffered violence at the hands of their partners and three-quarters have undergone female genital mutilation.

The power of culture to reinforce or revolutionize social and political attitudes should not be underestimated, not least for the way it operates on young and unconscious minds without needing to lecture or preach to them. I will never forget the positive effect that the 1998 Walt Disney animation *Mulan* seemed to have on my own son when he watched the film about the Chinese girl who disguises herself as a boy soldier to save her ageing father from conscription. With no prompting from me or particular discussion of the gender bending in the film, he immediately began to talk about the girls in his nursery as potential police officers and presidents. He was to some extent an embryonic observer of the cultural roles assigned to girls and women. Yet the most direct relationship between seeing power and becoming it must surely lie in the world of political media and its power to report, represent, distort, encourage or mask the contributions of women.

While there are some signs of progress, I have lost count of the times when first as an activist and 'expert' or later as a politician, I have been the only woman in the studio or on the panel. The problem is exacerbated by so much flagship news and political programming (in the UK at least) being anchored by and even named after men who understandably remain in such well-paid and prestigious professional homes for decades. I have been hectored, talked over and even given the occasional patronizing 'well done' in response to my answer to an interview question. I have walked into radio and TV studios with a male adversary, to watch him greeted like either a VIP or an old friend by our interviewer, while I am grudgingly welcomed or even ignored.

Recently I appeared on a one-hour current affairs programme in a prime-time television slot. I counted ten faces, including the presenter and newsreader (both men). Out of those ten, only two were women – me and one of the three newspaper reviewers. You could of course argue that the programme-makers were bound by the news agenda for the week. But the eight male voices included a Hollywood actor and the musician who sang at the end of the programme. Certain that this must have been an unhappy fluke, I looked back at the previous episode of the weekly magazine show. Again there had been ten voices in total. Again only two were women, and middle-aged white men filled both the actor interview and musical slots. The week before that, the programme managed three women in the form of two newspaper reviewers and the singer at the end of the show. So there was no woman interviewed in either a political or cultural slot and the overall air-time for the women was probably less than even their numbers might suggest. And so on and so on. On the rare occasions that parity was more or less achieved on this particular programme, it was only by way of two out of three newspaper reviewers and the musical slot being filled by women. It never seems to be achieved by way of the political interview slots.

And how easy this would be to change, especially in publicly funded broadcasting of the kind that I am describing but even in the commercial sphere (not least if the Geena Davis box-office statistics might translate from cinema to current affairs). Where is it written that talk shows should be anchored by men or that they cannot be co-presented by a man and a woman of equal experience, gravitas and prominence? I have certainly seen many able women journalists passed over for the plum jobs. Why should it not be a stated aim of such broadcasting that it broadly reflects society? And if the topical political interviews in any given week simply cannot include equal numbers of men and women, why should the newspaper reviewers, expert commentators, cultural and musical slots not be used to make up the difference?

Why on earth should any little girl watching current affairs TV – as I once did – even imagine a place for herself at the table? They say that at the age of seven an equal number of boys and girls in Western democracies want to lead their country, but that the proportion of girls drops drastically by the age of fifteen. The UN figures on the political representation of women worldwide make for sobering reading. In June 2016 just 22.8 per cent of members of national parliaments were women, marking a slow rise from 11.3 per cent over the previous twenty years. Rwanda had the highest percentage of women with 63.8 per cent in its lower house but there were thirty-eight states where women made up less than 10 per cent of a single or lower house and four chambers with no women at all. The data (provided by UN missions) showed wide regional variations in participation. The Nordic countries performed best with an average of 41.1 per cent in single, lower or upper houses. In the Americas the average was 27.7 per cent and in Europe (minus the Nordic countries) 24.3 per cent. Asia averaged 18.4 per cent female representation and the Pacific region 13.5 per cent. In January 2017 there were just ten women heads of state and nine women heads of government out of around 200 countries in the world. Ten years earlier a mere 17 per cent of government ministers worldwide were women, with most of these holding social policy briefs such as Education and Families. The UN statistics suggest that only Rwanda and Bolivia (53.1 per cent) had more than 50 per cent female representation as late as June 2016 and only forty-six countries had broken the 30 per cent barrier. Tellingly forty of the forty-six countries in the 30 per cent club had achieved this by some form of quota system, involving either quotas for candidates or reserved seats for women in the relevant parliament or assembly.

The UN research asserts that women have worked well across party lines, cooperating on issues such as gender-equality law, gender-based violence, parental leave and childcare provision. While it had no comprehensive numbers on local government participation, the UN cited evidence from India and Norway of a direct causal connection between greater female representation and the establishment of greater availability of drinking water and childcare provision respectively.

So what might the future look like and what means could and should accelerate progress in women's political representation? There is of course ample potential for progressive political parties to prioritize the issue both as a matter of principle and as vote-winning policy. Women-only shortlists can be employed in the selection of candidates in particular seats to boost female representation in the parliament or assembly. This tool has the advantage of being flexible enough not generally to require legislation, external influence or the cooperation of political forces beyond the party itself. On the other hand, women-only shortlists can give rise to a tension between a party's structures at national and local level and, at least in the short term, create resentment among men who feel a particular attachment to or stake in the area or constituency in question. It is also open to parties actively to seek out and recruit women as potential members with a view to mentoring and training them for electoral office and then to place greater numbers of them in any qualifying pool of candidates for subsequent selection. Again this involves considering equal representation an essential and integral component of the party's political mission and brand. Any kind of affirmative action brings the risk of resentment, which can only be countered with a firm narrative and clear mission as to why such measures are, for the time being at least, so needed. If gender equality is not seen as a core value of the political project in question, this is unlikely to succeed.

One could go further still. If the political consensus in an entire country or political community were for greater equality, one could seek legislative or even constitutional amendments on either a permanent or time-limited basis to kick-start fairer representation of women. Additional or top-up seats could be reserved in any parliamentary assembly, to be filled post-general election, on a regional or national electoral basis. This would of course break the usual geographical representative link and create two classes of parliamentarian with all the associated risks. A more radical but perhaps principled approach would be to create fewer but larger constituencies, each with a male and female representative and to give electors two votes – one for a candidate of each sex. I can almost hear the roars of laughter or anger as I write. These are times when even to dream of a different and fairer world invites the charge of 'political correctness gone mad'. But not so long ago, even the idea of women voting was considered just as outrageous to the social and political order. And one way or another, and as with women's suffrage itself, more equal representation will be advanced only with the help of male supporters of the cause, prepared to offer a hand of friendship in place of the hand of possession. So the moral case for affirmative action is one to which we must return.

3. Wealth and Production

How much are you worth? And for that matter, how much is the worth of everyone you do and don't know? What value do you place on the planet and everything on it? I wonder what you are thinking about right now. The state of your bank balance – if you are lucky enough to have one (according to the UN, over a billion women do not); any salary, savings or even property – if you have that privilege? Or my question might have provoked anxiety about piles of bills and mounting debt. Perhaps you are attempting to conjure up those incomprehensible sums held by multinational corporations that outstrip so many countries, or those gods on Olympus that feature in the *Forbes* Magazine Billionaires List. You may have heard that given the way that super-wealth begets super-wealth, the rate of widening inequality worldwide will probably produce its first trillionaire within the next twenty-five years. In case you are wondering, that is twelve noughts. Maybe instead you are thinking about your worth in terms of what you contribute or hope to contribute to the world, whether in the form of supporting your family, community, society or even posterity.

Yet, let's not dwell on this particular hypothetical for too long. These questions have long been settled and not by you or me. Furthermore, what is considered of most economic value and what constitutes or may be translated into things called private property and wealth, public finances or gross domestic product (GDP) is not for the most part female, nor in female hands. In very much earlier times of human existence, this may well have been at least a little different.

However, even this is now highly contested and often regarded as a kind of idealistic nostalgia that cannot imagine any brave or better way of living that hasn't at least somewhere and sometime been tried before. One thing is for certain though, in the early part of the twenty-first century, the bulk of the world's fragile and ever-dwindling resources and the 'golden tickets' to access them, sit in the hands of an extreme few. Most of them are men.

In 1907, Keir Hardie, the first leader of the British Labour Party, wrote as follows:

> In the United States of America, where capitalism has reached its fullest development, one per cent of the population owns ninety-nine per cent of the wealth.

An influential Oxfam report from January 2017, 'An economy for the 99%', cites President Obama's final address to the UN General Assembly in September 2016:

> A world where 1 per cent of humanity controls as much wealth as the bottom 99 per cent will never be stable.

Just eight men own as much as the 3.6 billion people who make up the poorest half of the human race. Seven out of ten people live in a country that has seen a rise in inequality over the last thirty years. Further, in the period between 1988 and 2011, incomes of the world's richest 1 per cent grew by $11,800. That is 182 times the $65 growth of the poorest 10 per cent. Oxfam goes on to predict that over the next twenty years 500 people will hand over $2.1 trillion to their heirs. That is more than the GDP of India with its 1.3 billion people. Contrary to convenient and complacent myth, most of the super-rich are far from 'self-made'.

Women find themselves disproportionately among the poorest on earth, on account of either overt or more subtle discrimination in the context of property rights, the labour market and professions, or because they shoulder a huge and disproportionate share of the domestic and caring responsibilities within the family, which are either treated as completely without monetary value or significantly under-resourced and rewarded. Unsurprisingly therefore, it is suggested that it will take 170 years for women to achieve even mere pay equality with men.

Yet the world would not function, nor humanity sustain itself without this unaccounted for private sphere of women giving birth to and nurturing each next generation of little workers, soldiers, leaders and reproducers of the same. So there can be no question that this kind of work is, or has ever really been regarded as, trivial. There is an ocean of culture, literature, advertising and even political polemic and propaganda spanning the world and the ages, urging women on to perform their duties as wives, mothers and daughters. It is just that this domestic labour should be performed – not so much on a zero hours contract – as for zero pay and diminishing status and security as life and time go on. And notwithstanding women's lesser participation in paid work, as late as 2015 the United Nations Statistics Division calculated that when housework and caring duties are taken into account alongside remunerated employment, women work a total average of thirty minutes a day longer than men in developed countries. This rises to fifty minutes more in the developing world.

The literary origins of the maxim that a woman's place is in the home are thought to be attributable to the Ancient Greek Aeschylus in 467 BC in the third of his Oedipus trilogy, *Seven Against Thebes*: 'Let women stay at home and hold their peace.'

Such sentiments ring across the globe and the centuries. They continue even and despite the development of a counter-narrative that has often accompanied times of revolution, war or more gradual change in attitudes. These triggers have allowed or required either a moral or practical re-evaluation of the desirability of an alternative role for women outside the home and family environment.

Henrik Ibsen's 1879 heroine Nora Helmer may as well have been the dramatic personification of the woman as perpetual child that Mary Wollstonecraft identified in her seminal *A Vindication of the Rights of Woman* nearly a century earlier in 1792. Nora's lack of either paid employment or personal property traps her in the state of middle-class marriage, tempts her into fraud and even the contemplation of suicide before she scandalizes her husband and nineteenth-century audiences by possibly leaving the family home to discover herself. Of course a great deal has changed in the last century and a half. But the change has been not nearly enough when it comes to women all over the world realizing their economic worth and potential, and the consequent independence and self-confidence, not to mention the greater security that this can bring for themselves and their children.

When domestic labour is performed unpaid – predominantly by women – it can seem invisible or at least go unrecognized. And however it is perceived and even appreciated by those who render and receive the services, it cannot be converted into anything that will buy independence, agency, security or prestige for the woman concerned. 'What have you been doing all day?' The phrase has surely been readily translatable across continents and time ever since a man brought a dead beast back for supper and a woman spent the day tending babies, fetching water and attempting to make fire (even if she had also killed a few beasts in her time). Of course I simplify – but not that much. As soon as labour is divided in communities and societies, primitive or modern, someone decides whose labour counts – and that someone is usually a man.

Work that is essential but unpaid becomes the greatest eater of time. In a finite human life, time is something that should be (and in very many respects is) of value. In the best traditions of both Hollywood and science fiction, while being gripping and not remotely worthy, the 2011 action movie *In Time* by Andrew Niccol really brings the point home. It features a moment in the latter part of the twenty-first century when people have been genetically engineered to stop ageing at twenty-five and are issued with only a year left to live. This is evidenced by the insertion of a digital clock on the forearm of each person. In this dystopian society time is the hard currency. People in poor neighbourhoods struggle to beg, borrow, steal and make ends meet with a matter of hours or even minutes in the bank, while their wealthy near-neighbours hoard centuries and seek to live for ever. I have rarely seen a better allegory for wealth inequality today or a more profound literal insight into the true value of time in the human experience. Translated into our own moment, women in developed countries spend an average of two hours per day more on unpaid work than men and three hours more in developing ones.

That great modern science (or is it perhaps more of a religion?) of economics has under-represented women both among its senior disciples and in its thinking, which has too often regarded women's domestic labour as a wholly 'non-economic phenomenon'. The scarcity of women economics professors is often remarked upon, as is the comment by Alfred Marshall – widely regarded as the father of neo-classical economics in the late nineteenth and early twentieth centuries – that economics is 'the study of men as they live and think and move in the ordinary business of life'. Yet in the same radical period that coincided with struggles for women's suffrage, in 1898 in the United States Charlotte Perkins Gilman was looking at economics in a way that didn't ignore female domestic labour and argued that it should be better shared or professionalized in the cause of greater independence for women (*Women and Economics – A Study of the Economic Relation Between Men and Women as a Factor in Social Evolution*).

This basic moral, political and economic argument was being remade and updated nearly a century later in 1988, by Marilyn Waring in her book *If Women Counted*, and she is now widely regarded as the modern-day founder of what is often described as 'feminist economics'. And yet in its concern for what is of real benefit to people, the planet and future generations, her contribution might just as easily be regarded as significant to 'human' and 'sustainable' economic thinking as opposed to the orthodoxy that either gently sugarcoats or aggressively justifies ever greater inequality between people and generations and hastens the death of the species and the planet. There are a host of definitions for a 'genius idea', but one of them must surely involve the thought that seems at once so dangerously radical and obviously truthful that it must have been hiding in plain view for thousands to walk past until its discoverer and advocate turned up. The idea that women's vital but unpaid home work should be accounted for in the GDP of nations was surely such an idea, for which we have Waring to thank. If only more nations would take her advice.

For it is not as if such industry doesn't count – and count considerably – when it is conducted for pay or profit. Imagine all the wages and dividends reaped from the manufacture and sale of domestic labour-saving white goods such as refrigerators, washing machines and dishwashers. Then there is the significant industry in private childcare, food and hospitality and paid domestic labour (even if these, when overly populated by women or migrant labour, can be undervalued around the world). If some of this work must be done without formal recompense within the home, it must be better shared by men and women. Further, the basic incomes and living conditions of these people and families must be better protected by society as a whole so as not to disadvantage unduly those who take on significant domestic or caring responsibilities. And there should surely be better provision for free and affordable childcare in a professionalized sector that better rewards the women and men who might increasingly want to work in it. Surely it is time to stop financially penalizing women who seek to work for both financial reward and personal fulfilment outside the home.

Sadly however, economic inequity does not end at the threshold nor even within the walls of the family home. In most societies, security and ownership of land have been thought critical to social and economic empowerment. Yet in thirty-four countries in the world daughters do not have the same inheritance rights as their brothers and in thirty-five, widows fail automatically to inherit their land and homes from their deceased husbands.

In January 2017, Monique Villa of the Thomson Reuters Foundation told the World Economic Forum that land and property form up to 75 per cent of a nation's wealth. Yet three-quarters of people in the world cannot prove that they own the land on which they live or work. Once more the position of women is the worst. Women farmers lack equal rights to own land in over ninety countries and 25 million urban women in the Middle East and North Africa lack equal constitutional and statutory property rights. Her most startling revelation is perhaps that 'women own less than 20 per cent of the world's land, yet more than 400 million of them farm and produce the majority of the world's food supply'. The average of 20 per cent of female land ownership is said to dip to as low as 10 per cent in a number of developing nations, though as Yale economist Cheryl Doss points out, the national variations and comparisons with men are interesting and important, as is the need for reliable and up-to-date data on ownership. Uganda seems to be a particular concern with a greater than 20 per cent disparity between the percentage of women and men owning agricultural land on even a joint basis. This is the inevitable result of a traditional lack of independent land ownership rights for women, the consequent need to negotiate with the family of a husband or former husband, and twenty years of conflict in that country.

Villa advocates land-titling reform as one way forward. Post-conflict Kosovo, where female ownership sits at around 15 per cent, is adopting this approach. Yet land-titling and indeed reform can surely benefit women only if combined with constitutional equality and both the political will and legal teeth with which to enforce it, even in the face of local and regional traditions, and even as a condition for aid and support from wealthier nations and international institutions.

Thus a disproportionate responsibility for unpaid domestic work and discrimination in ownership and inheritance will still hold a woman back to a greater or lesser extent all over the world. But the obstacle course she faces does not end there and continues well into the labour market and the world of work.

Work can be a wonderful thing. For many of us it brings dignity, industry, interest, company and belonging. It may also bring at least part of the means to feed, clothe, house, educate and amuse ourselves and any partners and dependents. I do not want to sentimentalize. Work can also involve boredom, frustration, indignity, exploitation and even grave injury when the relationship between employer and employee becomes too unequal or labour is otherwise viewed as cheap or disposable. Yet when societies and economies function well and in the interests of everyone, work can be an enormous net positive both spiritually and materially at a personal and community level. Without it, at least for many people, life can be a strange, frightening and even pointless journey. I am not saying that this is true for everyone or that paid work is always essential to a happy and healthy existence, but for most of us – women and men alike – it can certainly help.

The most important relationships of my own life outside my immediate birth family were found and forged either in education or the world of work. This may well reflect the urban background of the daughter of migrants, consequently lacking in long-term neighbours or extended family. I would venture to suggest, though, that even in less transient communities or rural ones where people grow up to know generations of their neighbours all their lives, collective work of whatever kind brings fruitful ties of friendship and solidarity.

So it seems worth reflecting on the 2015 statistics from the United Nations that while 77 per cent of men participate in the workforce globally, only half of the world's women enjoy the same privilege. The gap is thought to have narrowed in some regions since the UN Fourth World Conference on Women in Beijing in 1995, aimed at addressing equality, development and peace. And there has been a broad increase for women aged twenty-five and above (the years between twenty-five and fifty-four being considered the prime working age). However, the gender gap is particularly wide in

North Africa and Western and Southern Asia. Most worryingly, half of all global employment is considered of a 'vulnerable' nature, and while this is most common in Africa and Asia, it is always most common of all among women.

Unsurprisingly perhaps, women predominate in the provision of services such as education, health and social care (making their work, pay and conditions especially vulnerable to cuts in public spending in many countries). However, what the UN describes as 'occupational segregation' is to be found in all regions of the planet. Further, women earn less than men is all sectors and occupations: in most countries women working full-time earn between 70 and 90 per cent of what men earn. That is not a statistic I would like to have to explain to a classroom of bright-eyed and optimistic schoolgirls of whatever nationality or class anywhere.

More cheeringly, over half of all countries now provide at least fourteen weeks maternity leave (an offering that has increased over the last twenty years) and paternity leave has become more common. The UN suggests that, while only 27 per cent of countries offered this benefit as late as 1994, this rose to 48 per cent of countries by 2015. Shockingly, though, the United States of America still has no national statutory maternity or paternity leave at all. According to the US National Partnership for Women and Families, as of the beginning of 2017, 86 per cent of people employed in the American private sector had no access to paid maternity or paternity leave. Consequently, one in four new mothers were back at work within two weeks of giving birth. Surely this is not to be tolerated on either maternal health or infant development grounds in one of the wealthiest nations in the world.

The results of a ground-breaking Gallup–International Labour Organization (ILO) survey, 'Towards a better future for women and work', published on International Women's Day in March 2017, make for interesting and ultimately optimistic reading. The views of 149,000 adults in 142 countries were taken and demonstrate a coming together of opinion between the sexes around the world in favour of women engaging in paid work outside the home: 77 per cent of women and 66 per cent of men would prefer women to be in paid jobs and each figure is double that of those who would prefer women to stay at home. Further, the majority in favour includes a majority of women not currently in the workforce. Significantly, it is true of all regions of the planet, including those with a traditionally low female participation – such as Arab states.

To approach the question from a more cultural standpoint, most people the world over (85 per cent of women and 81 per cent of men) believe that it is 'acceptable' for women to work outside the home, and even in North Africa, where the views of women and men are farthest apart, 79 per cent of women and 57 per cent of men agree. These figures are lower in families with children and those where the wider family does not approve of women in employment. 'Work–family balance' is seen as a challenge for working women everywhere. However, there are more significant variations in concern about unfair treatment at work (perceived as a greater problem in the developing world), lack of child and social care (more acute in developing and emerging nations) and unequal pay (a bigger concern in the developed world).

One particularly interesting finding is that the more highly educated a woman, the less likely she is to perceive better opportunities for women in the workplace. By contrast, the views of men tend not to change very much based on their education. Further, a woman's challenges change with age and circumstance. Young women twenty-nine and under are more likely to mention unfair treatment, abuse or harassment at work. Women aged between thirty and forty-four are more likely than those in other age groups to cite the lack of affordable care for their children and families. It is women over forty-four who seem to become most acutely aware of unequal pay.

Finally, physical security travelling to and from work (especially at night) is a concern the world over. No matter how objectively unsafe the region (respondents in Latin America and the Caribbean feel the least safe walking home at night), men always feel safer than women. The disparity in this perceived safety between men and women in different regions fluctuates between about 5 and 16 per cent.

First, therefore, we must address the question of women's genuine freedom to participate at all. We have already looked at the worldwide barrier of childcare and other unpaid duties. However, in a country like Saudi Arabia, discrimination is so draconian that prohibitions on women driving and associating with men create an overt, formal and virtually physical block on a great deal of employment options. In many other countries, the obstacles may be less formal but nonetheless significant in terms of lack of educational opportunity, transport, protection from violence and other vital infrastructure that can facilitate access to work. These must be addressed as a matter of political priority and public investment if women are to stand a chance of getting to meaningful work.

Where employment is vulnerable, it should be protected or, at the very least, less vulnerable models should be developed by governments or ethical business or social enterprise. The idea that insecure employment benefits the economy by driving down wages should surely be consigned to a barbaric past. One simply cannot improve the lot of working women without ensuring and enforcing decent employment conditions, such as protection from discrimination on grounds of sex and maternity and some reasonable level of wage and workplace security.

The world of work is highly segregated both horizontally and vertically along gendered lines. So even a woman who gains access to paid employment is more than likely to do so in traditionally and stubbornly 'female' employment that is characterized by low pay and status, long hours and part-time or informal (including non-taxed) working arrangements. Such work may suit childcare needs in the short term, but is likely to fail to deliver on work or financial security or progression for the woman and her family in the long run. This pattern is replicated globally and seems particularly intractable, perhaps because in the light of other forms of injustice (including other forms of gender injustice), concentrations of men and women in different parts of the labour market can seem more of a quirky cultural phenomenon than a social evil.

Yet it is a social and economic evil nonetheless. Firstly, female-dominated areas of employment will inevitably attract lower pay and status than those in which men predominate or which have become more mixed. The idea of man as breadwinner persists in the public and private sectors as excuse or even justification for discriminatory pay policy. Secondly, such segregation is in itself a result of either self-selection based on centuries of stereotyping and muted ambition, or of discrimination in national law or in the employment sectors in which women are thinner on the ground. According to the World Bank Group report 'Women, Business and the Law' in 2016, at least one hundred states (including Russia and Argentina) still actually barred women from certain types of work with dangerous substances or machinery in industry and agriculture. Many others effectively bar them by the lack of anti-discrimination provision. Thirdly, and because so many of the sectors in which women predominate are of a caring nature (teaching and nursing), effectively to continue to downgrade their status and reward is to warp societies' values and the messages they send to each new generation. To take pre-school childcare and primary education as an example, what story does a country tell its children if their care and education – even outside the home – is overwhelmingly provided by women? What signal to small boys in particular? And in the light of so many fluid and even fatherless families across the globe, imagine the benefits of positive social policy intervention to attract more men into this kind of work.

Mira Nair's 2016 film *Queen of Katwe* is worth watching with this and so much more in mind. At first sight, it is the wonderfully inspiring story of the young Phiona Mutesi (played by Madina Nalwanga), who rises from some of the most difficult conditions imaginable – Katwe is a slum of Kampala, Uganda – to become a chess prodigy. She educates herself and thus manages to lift her mother and siblings out of abject urban poverty and day-to-day insecurity as to food and shelter. Yet the undercurrent of the film makes it so much more than a feminist *Karate Kid* for the twenty-first century. Two understated themes of the story are the enormous influence of HIV/AIDS on so many African societies (Phiona and her siblings are fatherless and her mother left without any economic security as a result of their father's death of AIDS), and the enormous potential for modern masculinity to learn from conflict and loss and to redefine itself as the nurturer, educator and leader of children – girls and boys. Phiona's chess coach Robert Katende (played with aplomb by David Oyelowo) is perhaps the secret weapon of the movie. Orphaned through the Ugandan turmoil of his own childhood, he takes up a very modern and relevant form of Christian mission (even at the expense of better paid, more secure and prestigious employment) to teach productive struggle and strategy to the most vulnerable children in his country. As so often, popular culture in general and cinema in particular can prove both more subtle and powerful agents for a change in attitudes than exhortation, polemic and law in isolation.

In March 2016 the International Trade Union Confederation (ITUC) published a gender analysis of employment stimulus in seven OECD countries (Australia, Denmark, Germany, Italy, UK, Japan and US). 'Investing in the Care Economy' (prepared by the Women's Budget Group) makes a powerful case for public investment in infrastructure in times of economic recession and for changing our thinking and accounting rules so that 'social infrastructure' counts alongside physical infrastructure projects such as the building of bridges and roads. Social infrastructure is defined as caring services such as healthcare, education, childcare and adult long-term care (e.g. of the elderly). The report begins by restating the important argument that investing in employment that provides a public good is a far better approach than cutting the taxes of the wealthy in difficult economic times. Greater employment and household income stimulates demand in the economy generally. By contrast, delivering tax cuts at the top will lead to the hoarding of wealth and quite possibly to economic stagnation as opposed to the sharing of wealth or any other consequential societal benefits. The report goes on to argue, though, that while a 2 per cent of GDP investment in either the construction or caring industries would create considerable new employment in all the countries in the study, investment in care is particularly advantageous. It creates more employment (being labour rather than material intensive) and reduces gender inequality (as more women work in the sector and others who benefit from it may be then freed up to work elsewhere). Further, even though the construction and care industries are both gendered, there is still more of an even split in the world of care.

Other initiatives are no doubt required in a whole host of sectors where women have failed to break through. I believe that governments and legislatures should explore allowing employers in highly segregated sectors to discriminate positively in favour of applicants from the under-represented sex. Sometimes this could be specifically endorsed on the basis of either social good or the benefit to the industry or profession. Sometimes it could be incentivized by government grants or tax relief. Sometimes, where the shortage of one sex (usually women) is said to present a particular societal problem, such affirmative action could and should be required by law.

Horizontal or sector-based segregation is far from the whole story of discrimination in the world of work. Think about cooking, clothes-making and hairdressing. Most of this activity in the world is surely performed by women in or outside the home. Yet when it becomes a matter of high market value, pay or prestige, the starred chef, designer or hairdresser is most likely a man. Once more, some of this will be an overt culture of sexism or the way that the workplace or work pattern is organized. Some of it will be that subliminal but no less constant message in a young or even older woman's mind that this or that kind of aspiration or role is 'simply not for someone like me'. Again I think that so-called vertical segregation, whether caused by women self-selecting themselves out of the race for promotion or by discriminatory employers, should be consciously addressed by state, corporate and consumer action.

Segregation in the labour market is only the beginning of this story, though. Discrimination arises at every stage of the employment process, from seeking work to workplace practices and behaviours, remuneration, promotion and job security. Even where countries have clear and long-standing anti-discrimination laws in place, too much onus can be placed on an individual employee to enforce those laws, without access to adequate information (for instance, about relative pay in an organization) or practical recourse to advice and redress. How many of us would actually put ourselves through the pain of suing an employer if we had not actually been dismissed unfairly and in the absence of some huge safety or corruption scandal that must be exposed in the public interest? The most exquisite employment protection and anti-discrimination laws can be a dead letter in a sealed book without a degree of both transparency and solidarity in the workplace.

The gender pay gap is the perfect example of this problem. The International Labour Organization introduced the Equal Remuneration Convention in 1951, President Kennedy signed the Equal Pay Act in the USA in 1963 and the UK introduced the Equal Pay Act in 1970. Since then, very many states the world over have brought forward constitutional and statutory measures outlawing pay discrimination between men and women. And yet the World Economic Forum reported in 2016 that women were being paid almost half of male pay globally and that the combined gap in income and employment had widened, with women at 59 per cent of male attainment – a similar level to that during the worst times of the financial crisis in 2008. It seems more than clear that exhortations and even equal pay laws can have no teeth without positive obligations on employers to provide transparency in pay policy, for example by auditing gender pay gaps and publishing the results. Nation states have corporate auditing requirements and taxing agencies to investigate taxable profits and liability. It would seem logical that equal pay obligations could be made a similar priority with the corresponding auditing, investigation and enforcement powers given to the government agencies currently responsible for corporate governance or tax or other regulatory obligations. Why should not company auditors and tax inspectors look at the equal pay performance of employers as well as their other governance and tax responsibilities?

Very occasionally, visionary people – including employers – act upon conscience and values without being threatened by the levers of either audit, litigation or collective employee action. My friend and former colleague Professor Anthony Forster, the Vice-Chancellor of the University of Essex, is one of these. In the summer of 2016, having audited university pay differentials, Anthony took the bold and unprecedented step of putting the institution's money quite literally where its mouth had been for some time. He made a positive, though some would say expensive, one-off pay uplift intervention to redress a differential that had developed over time in male and female professorial pay. This is what he said at the time:

> I have been asked why have we taken this action now, when no other university has taken this step? For us, this decision is about living up to our own University's values which make clear the importance of a diverse and inclusive environment in which we treat our members with equal respect and dignity. This means that we should be rewarding people in a fair and transparent way, based upon their contribution to our community regardless of their personal characteristics.

Frustratingly, this progressive approach is the exception not the rule. In the UK, the gender pay gap according to most recent estimates is 18.1 per cent with many institutions, in both the private and public sectors, fostering gender pay disparity. A 2016 policy designed to promote transparency obliged the British public service broadcaster, the BBC, to publish salaries above £150,000 a year, paid for by the television licence fee. The figures revealed a staggering gender pay gap. Of the corporation's top earners, only one third were women and the highest-earning four male presenters across the BBC were collectively paid four times the total paid to the four top female presenters. Happily, the gender inequality revealed by the publication of BBC pay data provoked outrage and real debate about equality in the workplace. It remains to be seen if this will translate into more robust action. Instituting women Time Lords is a wonderful thing, but surely they should be paid the same as their male peers?

Individual and legislative action notwithstanding, no discussion of the struggle for workplace equality and greater security – past, present or future – would be complete without considering the decisive role of trade unions around the world. Inequality between the world's haves and have-nots would never have been challenged, however frustratingly incompletely and inconsistently, without the organizing of labour from the 1800s on.

Given that women are at the bottom of the pile of world labour, it is hardly surprising that ever more of them are seeking to organize in the changing global world of work. The International Trade Union Confederation was founded in November 2006 as a result of a merger between two existing confederations. It quickly prioritized women, whether in its own ranks, the workplace or the wider world, and published a manual, *Achieving Gender Equality*, in January 2008.

It reported that more women were joining unions than ever before, and that they were beginning to overtake men in membership. In 1949 only seven out of a hundred union members were women as opposed to four out of ten globally by 2008.

This dramatic change in the ratio of women to men trade unionists was attributed to the number of women in well-unionized public sectors, a corresponding decline in membership in male-dominated manufacturing, greater gender awareness and expansion into the services industries, alongside success in recruitment into new and previously unorganized employment on the part of even traditional trade unions. Continued progress of this kind seems to be key to both the advancement of women in work and the continuing relevance and progress of trade unions as a workplace, community, national and international influence for dignity and equality in the world.

The inherent nature of inequality in the relationship between employers and employees requires the balancing effect of collective bargaining as to terms and conditions of work, as well as vital support in the case of disputes involving individual workers. At national level, unions have been instrumental in securing such minimum standards as exist, including in relation to workplace safety and anti-discrimination. Further, the international nature of trade unionism has often been a powerful lever for even the humblest of workers to achieve real change in the world. In the 1980s, young Irish supermarket cashiers helped build momentum for the boycott against fruit from apartheid South Africa. In many minds, the paradigm of trade union power lies in industrial action and ultimately strike action in the face of a dispute. However, in the context of vulnerable workers, and women in particular, union lawyers and negotiators can be a vital resource for both worker and employer when appropriate understanding and remedy are required in relation to workplace discrimination and even harassment between employees.

That said, there are two obvious challenges to the role of unions as an agent for gender justice in the contemporary world. The first lies in the rise of disparate, remote and even international workforces and informal arrangements which are often deliberately designed to circumvent employment contracts, legal protection and workplace solidarity. However, there is ample evidence of modern trade unions rising to this challenge as is demonstrated by union-backed litigation against the 'non-employment' and low-tax arrangements of global brands such as Uber, and by successful solidarity with and even recruitment among technically 'self-employed' people. Distinctions between 'public' and 'private', 'employed' and 'self-employed' become less and less real in the globalized world of work. If abusive state or corporate employers seek to 'divide and rule' by subcontracting services and undercutting wages, working women will often be the losers. So unions must increasingly reach out across these divides and innovate in other ways to re-create the power of the collective. The Self Employed Women's Association (SEWA) is India's largest union with 2 million members in a female labour force that is 94 per cent self-employed. It helps to educate and finance its members (via its own cooperative bank), in addition to assisting with health, childcare and legal advice.

A second challenge lies in changing the nature of representation and the conduct of business within trade unions themselves. Even in unions where women's membership has surged or overtaken that of men, there often remains a lack of women in representative positions, especially at the highest levels. Trade unions around the world are attempting to speed up progress in this area with a range of tactics, including actively recruiting and training women to become organizers and leaders within the movement. The history of trade unions as educators as well as organizers of working people is a long and noble one with a new urgency and relevance in the internet age. Some create women's committees in which to begin the process of identifying the most relevant issues and building women's confidence in advocacy and leadership – an approach that has proved popular in countries as far apart as Japan, Zimbabwe and the UK. Many unions monitor gender balance at all levels and now employ affirmative and constitutional action to achieve greater involvement at a senior level. I cannot place enough emphasis on the importance of trade unions being the most inclusive and representative environment possible for women. Old-fashioned, overly formal and pedantic meetings where the long-initiated trade 'points of order' into the night will not attract the precious interest and involvement of women (no doubt worried about getting home). Yet these women are and must increasingly be the heads, hearts and faces of the trade union movement worldwide.

As the priorities of India's SEWA suggest, access to banking and finance is a crucial feature of coming out of poverty and securing a more stable and successful economic life anywhere in the world. But this is far from straightforward for millions of people whose lack of literacy, low income and poor infrastructure renders them either undesirable or unreachable for too many financial institutions. The advent of 'micro-finance' initiatives has been both celebrated and criticized in recent times. By 2012 Andhra Pradesh, an Indian state containing 6 per cent of the population, was thought to have 25 per cent of the country's micro-credit and

9.2 million defaulters. A spate of suicides two years earlier was allegedly linked to the country's largest provider, SKS Microfinance, which had publicly floated at a value of $1.5 billion. There were tales of overly enthusiastic lending built on staff incentives and the harassment and public shaming of defaulters, including by other borrowers. A micro-finance concept that had begun as almost a branch of philanthropy, was now viewed by many as having morphed into the most unattractive type of usury.

There is no doubt that providing even small loans as seed-corn investment in the modest start-up enterprises of rural and urban women can prove enormously empowering. However, as with any kind of financial service, regulation is key. Banking can support people and economies – locally, nationally and internationally – but it can also bring them to their knees, as we all saw so dramatically in 2008. Loans must be viable at fair interest rates. If they are provided for investment in a business, there should be real due diligence as to its potential. There should be provision for savings as well as borrowing. Crucially, banking will not empower a woman who is not in reality free to make financial decisions for herself. Twenty-first-century states should seek to achieve the greatest financial literacy and inclusion by providing various models of not-for-profit or mutual banking services to the poorest, who might otherwise be left to the loan-sharks or to drown. Girls and boys should be taught about money and finance as soon as they learn to count.

Ethical finance and investment are no less important in empowering highly skilled women in developed countries to create new businesses that might go on to employ many more of the same. In April 2017, the *Economist* considered the sexism of Silicon Valley (both Uber and Google have been accused of discrimination in workplace practices), reporting on a survey which showed 60 per cent of women working there had experienced unwanted sexual advances and two-thirds felt excluded from important work-related opportunities. There are about 15 per cent fewer women working at executive level in US tech than in other industries and the women are paid less than the men. While the journal took due account of the problem that too few women study science, technology, engineering and mathematics (the STEM subjects) at degree level, it made serious charges against the culture and practice of cliquey and male-dominated venture capitalism:

> Plenty of studies show that diverse teams are more productive. Hiring more women in venture capital seems to increase the odds of finding and funding those elusive female entrepreneurs.

The lot of women fund managers is equally depressing. According to investment research by Morningstar in 2016, across fifty-six countries, only one in five fund managers was a woman, with that percentage having declined since the financial crisis of 2008. The position of women was better in smaller markets such as Singapore, Portugal, Spain, Hong Kong and France and worse in larger ones including the UK. The US and Germany had the worst female inclusion rates with 10 per cent and 9 per cent respectively. This contrasts dramatically with other highly skilled categories of the global workforce such as doctors. In September 2016, 34 per cent of physicians in the US were thought to be women. In January 2017 the American Bar Association Commission on Women in the Profession reported 36 per cent female representation. Sadly this does not translate to the highest echelons. For at least twenty years around half of new entrants to the US legal fraternity have been women and yet, as late as 2015, nearly three-quarters of law firm partners were white men.

Whether or not one can categorically prove the greater productivity or lesser insularity of diverse teams (and there is a great deal of evidence to suggest one can), in some areas of working life the case for representative diversity goes beyond performance and justice for those directly involved. It becomes a matter of broader legitimacy and public trust. I would argue that this is true of all the regulated professions and, in particular, of the board rooms responsible for corporate governance and the judiciary responsible for maintaining the Rule of Law all over the world.

Judicial independence from political and other forms of power militates against the election of judges in a democracy built upon the precondition and foundation of the Rule of Law. However, this does not mean that the vital institution of the courts can be complacent in the face of calls for greater demographic representation and diversity. I would argue quite the contrary. In politically turbulent times of the kind being faced all over the world in the first part of the twenty-first century, judicial legitimacy and public trust in this vital limb of any modern constitution are arguably more important than ever – even more so when judges regrettably come under political or media attack. As referees of any constitution and of the wider public and private dealings that we have with each other, our judges must have our trust and support. Of course it is possible for a man to do justice for a woman and vice versa, but a markedly unrepresentative judiciary will ultimately fail to command the depth and breadth of popular respect that it needs, especially when it speaks truth to power or merely says the difficult thing in difficult times.

In October 2016 the Council of Europe published data on the proportion of women judges within its territories. The position of the UK was less than laudable. True enough, Azerbaijan could muster only 11 per cent women judges of its total bench. Northern Ireland, Scotland and England and Wales (separate legal jurisdictions) could manage only 23 per cent, 23 per cent and 30 per cent respectively. This stood in contrast with a 51 per cent average of women judges across the entire Council of Europe. Until July 2017, with the appointment of The Rt Hon Lady Justice Black, only one of the eleven justices of the UK Supreme Court was a woman: Baroness Brenda Hale of Richmond was the first (appointed as a Law Lord in 2006) and the only woman ever to have served in the highest court in the kingdom. This stood in marked and embarrassing contrast with three out of eight women in the US Supreme Court and the record of senior judiciaries all over the common law world. Similarly, only one in five judges of the High Court of England and Wales were women and only 23 per cent of the Court of Appeal. By contrast, 33 per cent of US judges at state and federal level were women.

Excuses for this state of affairs are often frankly embarrassing and a disservice to every defender of the UK legal system and its responsiveness, resilience and relevance over time. Where such excuses are not embarrassing they move into the realm of insult to the intelligence of half the population. The suggestion that 'diversity' and 'merit' are in competition for judicial appointments fails to understand their interconnectedness when selecting people who must quite literally sit in judgement over others. It also implies that the status quo with its deeply entrenched discrimination is somehow 'meritocratic'. I would argue that just as with democratic representation in legislatures, the demographic legitimacy of the independent judiciary anywhere in the world cannot be ignored. Where gradualist progress, such as wider recruitment pools, encouragement and mentoring of under-represented candidates, has not succeeded or not done so at a fast enough rate, forms of affirmative action must be adopted, even if this requires legislative or constitutional change. These can begin with greater transparency of data relating to appointments and move into aspirational targets that can be monitored and scrutinized by the public and polity. In the final analysis, I believe that the cause of human rights and the Rule of Law favours time-limited quotas of say 35 to 45 per cent of any modern judiciary in order to kick-start any much needed change.

Corporate governance is another crucial seat of power with enormous influence over the lives of everyone from shareholders to employees, contractors and consumers, and indeed everyone else with whom they share the natural resources and environment of the planet. Some multinationals are arguably more powerful than national governments and yet too many remain bastions of unrepresentative and largely male privilege. In 2015, and looking at over 3,000 global companies, Credit Suisse found that only 14.7 per cent of board seats were held by women, which did at least represent a 54 per cent increase since 2010. A number of nations require the boards of large or public companies to contain a proportion of women directors as a matter of law. Norway adopted such an approach in 2003 (legislating for a 40 per cent quota of women on the boards of public limited companies). There are now also quota provisions in Belgium, France, Germany, Iceland, Israel, Italy and Spain. In 2015, the European Commission reported that the greatest progress among its member states in the previous ten years had been in countries with legislative quotas, or where such affirmative action had at least been actively considered and debated.

I am ultimately an optimist and have always tried to be one, even in adversity. Policies for greater equality in general and greater redistribution of wealth and power in particular, may still seem heresy in many quarters. Yet I see them increasingly gaining greater currency in others – including in modern ethical business. In the end, I believe that women and men the world over will be better off when the top tables of power are more diverse and the gap between them and those lower down is substantially smaller. Corporations are now often richer than many governments and too many of them constantly seek to force down both wages and tax; some would prefer to dodge tax altogether in so-called 'havens'. Women are under-represented at most top seats of influence and over-represented among the poorest in the world, including those on low wages or no wages at all. This unlocked and underdeveloped power and potential of half of humanity is a great natural resource. All we really need is the imagination and courage to unleash it.

4. Health and Reproduction

After I completed fifty years in the noble profession of
women's health, I was once asked what is the one
prescription which I think women need most for their
health. My answer was 'power'. Power is what women
need to enjoy their right to health. Powerlessness of
women, in my professional experience, is a serious
health hazard, and particularly in maternal health. But
women have to fill that prescription themselves and to
keep a sustainable supply of it. No pharmacy will
dispense it for them. When asked about the dose, my
advice was to take as much as you get. There is no risk
of over-dosage, and there are no reported side effects.
— Professor Mahmoud F. Fathalla

A doctor's handwriting was never so clear and eloquent in
providing both medical and political diagnosis and a prescription for improving the condition of women and the
unenviable position of their overall 'health' in the world.
This internationally recognized obstetrician, gynaecologist
and legendary women's health rights' advocate has worked in
the field since the early 1960s.

My story begins even earlier. In 1948, out of the ashes of
the Second World War, nation states and the people they
served were coming together in an attempt to fashion a new
and progressive consensus built upon international institutions and universal values. The World Health Organization

(WHO) was one such institution. In its constitution it chose to define 'health' as 'a state of complete physical, mental and social well-being and not merely the absence of disease or infirmity'. This definition is all the more powerful for the way in which it pits the aspirational value against the bare minimum standard so as explicitly to choose the first. Yet by any stretch of reporting or imagination, almost seventy years on, neither the aspirational nor the minimal standard of health is being delivered to the vast majority of women.

Polly Clayden is an unassuming and at first glance even unlikely human rights hero. But a hero she is nonetheless. She sits opposite me in a simple family Thai restaurant in South London and sums up the problem with women's health worldwide:

A lot of women's health issues are not biological because women are pretty fit.

Like all good raconteurs, she instinctively pauses while I try to catch up with the apparent contradiction. Women's health? Not biological? What on earth can she mean? Surely it all boils down to women's vulnerabilities around the reproductive process and all that goes with them from sexual violence and female genital cutting, to lack of autonomy and maternal mortality? Then the crisp ringing English vowels return to remind me that, whether it is baby boys being held longer on the breast, women feeding their families before themselves or men taking priority with the new clean needle in intravenous recreational drug use, 'men go first'.

Clayden's is a fascinating story of international activism and the triumph of the human spirit. Polly went to art school in the 1980s, and like her peers loved style, fashion and music. She worked as a stylist in the first wave of music videos and enjoyed clubbing with her friends. Then the HIV/AIDS epidemic began. She found herself going to fewer gigs and too many funerals of people she knew. So she became involved in campaigns to support the development of and access to effective antiretroviral (anti HIV) treatment, and the provision of information and advice for HIV positive people. In her own words, the artist became 'seduced by the science' in search of the 'happy endings' that she confesses a yearning for. And with time, science and activism, those happy endings did eventually come. Twenty years after Polly Clayden's accidental entry into the world of public health, she has friends who have lived positive lives with HIV for all that time. 'It's not usually AIDS that troubles them now,' she tells me with an infectious grin. 'It's age.' At the same time, Polly is now a recognized international public health expert and the co-founder of HIV i-base, a treatment activist group that works with HIV positive people and medical professionals globally. It was her HIV work that took her into the world of women's health, paediatric care and the prevention of mother-to-child transmission.

For it had become increasingly clear that what had at first seemed to be an epidemic predominantly affecting gay men in the global north was to become a massive problem for women and children in the south and in Africa in particular. And this too often is a result of the risky behaviour of male partners and fathers. According to the WHO, three decades into the AIDS epidemic, it is young women who have the most new HIV infections in the world. This also makes them vulnerable to tuberculosis, which has become one of the leading causes of death among women aged between twenty and fifty-nine years of age in low-income countries.

The challenge of sexually transmitted infection (STI) does not end there. Human papillomavirus (HPV) is currently the most common STI in the world, and it is thought that most people will have the infection at some point in their life. As most infection causes no symptoms and goes with time, it is easy to pass on and difficult to detect. More concerning is its link to cervical cancer. It is suggested that as many as 70 per cent of cases were caused by HPV. Cervical and breast cancers are the most common cancers among women. They each kill half a million women every year, mostly in low- and middle-income countries, where there is little or no screening, prevention and treatment. It is now advised that eleven-year-olds should be vaccinated against HPV, though this predictably arouses considerable displeasure from those who see the preaching of abstinence as a complete and preferred alternative to the application of science. Just as importantly, however, all of this provision requires public health programmes, facilities and money. Then there is the big three of gonorrhoea, chlamydia and syphilis. They may sound like Shakespearean princesses, but are actually common STIs that can either pass without much note, cause considerable discomfort or result in much more significant health problems later on. Untreated syphilis leads to 200,000 stillbirths and early foetal deaths every year and the deaths of a further 90,000 newborn.

If Professor Fathalla is right that power is the strongest medicine for women's health, most experts agree that it is most effectively administered via education and political participation. Education is both essential for that subsequent participation and crucial to delivering some basic and life-saving and enhancing messages about how to live a healthy life, potentially to the full extent of the original WHO ideal. Comprehensive Sexuality Education (CSE) can form a key component of this aspect of public health policy and is defined by UNESCO as an 'age-appropriate, culturally relevant approach to teaching about sexuality and relationships by providing scientifically accurate, realistic, nonjudgemental information'.

Yet here lies the rub. Scientific accuracy, realism and nonjudgement remain far too controversial as basic principles in many parts of the world, or at least as far as sexuality and reproductive health are concerned. So a lack of consensus, policy and uniform standards across many nations has often left a vacuum to be filled by community and civil society for good or ill. In 2014, the Indian Minister of Health and Family Welfare, Dr Harsh Vardhan, floated the possible banning of 'so-called sex education'. He had previously caused a similar stir by advocating marital fidelity over the use of condoms in the fight against AIDS. However, his comments about sex education resonate with others in his country and well beyond, who believe that providing information somehow leads to earlier sexual activity and promiscuity.

Practice in the United States is far from consistent, with states differing dramatically in their approach to 'abstinence-only' until marriage versus safe-sex teaching and inclusive approaches to differing types of sexuality. Some even question whether classes should involve demonstrating the correct way to use condoms. There are legal bans in some states relating to teaching the 'intricacies' of sex or acceptability of same-sex relationships. 'Abstinence-only' is an approach that has received tens of millions of dollars of federal government funding in recent years, and there are a number of rather terrifying coaches (often middle-aged women) whose mission it is to preach the evils of sex outside wedlock, and to portray those (especially young women) who have engaged in it as soiled and damaged goods, ruined for life and marriage thereafter. I would never advocate premature sexual activity, promiscuity or attempting to separate the notions of sexual and emotional health among young people. But it does seem to me that, as in most areas of life, education and empowerment are a better recipe for achieving health and happiness than fear and self-loathing. While the increased overall prevalence of 'sex ed' teaching seems to be leading to less young teenage sexual activity in the US than in the 1980s, surveys conducted by the Centers for Disease Control and Prevention suggest that teenagers in 2013 were less likely to report using a condom than ten years earlier.

Nonetheless, UNESCO notes that the international evidence is of CSE having a positive impact on sexual and reproductive health worldwide, contributing towards reducing STIs, HIV and unintended pregnancy. Furthermore, sex education does not hasten sexual activity and can actually delay it. It has a positive impact on safer sexual behaviour and crucially on increased condom use.

Notwithstanding political and cultural controversy around sex education in India, the high rates of teenage pregnancy and sexual abuse in the country have prompted a number of civil society – including youth-led – programmes to develop and provide accurate, realistic and non-judgemental education with a particular focus on gender equality and consent.

Latin America is a part of the world where traditional macho attitudes have led to high rates of violence against women and pregnancy among girls under fourteen. Yet in Nicaragua, there is little sex education in school. In May 2017, Abby Young-Powell described the situation in the *Guardian* newspaper, citing the regional director of the UN Population Fund, Alvaro Serrano:

If an eleven-year-old girl arrives in hospital pregnant, nobody says anything ... Women and girls are dying because of poor sex education.

The response of the NGO Plan International has been led by the ideas of young women in devising and delivering a programme of school-based workshops for fifteen- to nineteen-year-old boys. These are aimed at getting them to think about men, women and intimate relationships from a perspective of equality.

A common denominator of successful programmes worldwide seems to be the attempt at combining good science and research with youth-led communication that is neither too late nor too overly abstract. It is better to communicate no-nonsense practical human biology in the context of real-life pressures and relationships.

The International Planned Parenthood Federation (IPPF) is a global leader in the field, and has achieved some real success in places like Kyrgyzstan in the eastern reaches of the former Soviet Union. Abby Young-Powell describes the problem of old Soviet distrust of modern contraception combining with religious influences to make sex education a 'taboo subject' despite being officially part of the curriculum. Here, twenty-year-old student volunteers have been found to be the most effective communicators to talk to fourteen- and fifteen-year-olds about pregnancy, STIs, contraception and sexuality.

Elsewhere, the internet and mobile phone technology can help address the challenges of more socially conservative societies (in, for example, the Arab world), or the geographical challenges of remote and rural communities or both. Education as a Vaccine (EVA) works in Nigeria, where it is thought that as many as one in three eighteen-year-olds already have a child or are pregnant. Abstinence is the official state sex-education policy and issues of contraception, consent, gender equality and LGBT sexuality are not addressed. EVA created an anonymous question and answer service delivered via telephone, text message, email and social media in order to provide young people with a means of discussing and learning about sexual and reproductive health and HIV/AIDS. The service has proved incredibly popular with users ranging between the ages of ten and thirty.

There can be little doubt as to the vital role of education in better health for everyone, but in the case of women and girls their own bodies (or rather societies' lack of care and respect for them) can provide an impediment even to accessing that education. It may be hard to believe, but there are still places in our world where prevailing prejudice around menstruation, or poverty and a lack of free or affordable feminine hygiene products, can put girls and women in a position of physical incapacity, degradation and even danger every month.

It would seem that no part of the world has the monopoly of virtue when it comes to mystification, suspicion and revulsion around women's periods. It was not so long ago that women in Italy were discouraged from making pasta sauce when menstruating, and English women thought that if they baked during their period the bread or cake would be less likely to rise. Some orthodox religious practice of different denominations promotes the idea of menstrual blood being somehow poisonous and of women being 'unclean' during their periods and thus required to stay away from holy places or abstain from certain aspects of observance. The practice of *chhaupadi* in parts of Nepal seems particularly extreme, when viewed through twenty-first-century eyes.

Roshani Tiruwa was fifteen and in the ninth grade at Rastara Bhasah Secondary School. Boys and girls of her age the world over were no doubt worrying about their schoolwork, friendships, appearance and most likely plenty of other things besides. Yet Roshani had the further misfortune of being an adolescent girl in Nepal's hilly Achram Province, where the practice of *chhaupadi* remains rife. This despite it having been outlawed by the Supreme Court of her country in 2005, which then issued a further directive against it in 2008. *Chhaupadi* is the tradition of isolating girls and women during menstruation and immediately after childbirth. It rests upon the understanding that there is something somehow toxic or unclean about menstrual blood that might stop cows from milking, crops from growing, make menfolk and livestock unwell and displease the gods if these bleeding females are not put in a form of crude quarantine for at least five to seven days. During this time, they are excluded from normal life, their usual diet and contact with males, and are made to sleep in cattle-sheds or other outhouses, alone and extremely vulnerable. Many women had already been lost to this cultural norm when Roshani crawled into a tiny hut having said goodnight to family members on the third day of her period in December 2016. It is thought that many others put through this exclusion before her had been attacked by wild animals, bitten by snakes or raped and murdered by neighbours or strangers. Newborn infants taken for the night with their new mothers had sometimes died of pneumonia. In Roshani's case, it was suspected that she suffocated to death, having lit a small fire for warmth in the tiny shelter which was to become her tomb. In August 2017, and after yet more deaths of young women, the Nepalese Parliament finally passed a law banning *chhaupadi*, but now backed with criminal sanctions of up to three months in prison or a fine. However, the law was set to come into force a year later. So only time will tell whether it can be matched with sufficient public education and enforcement resources to make a real difference.

It is easy to feel sadness followed by anger at this apparently backward, barbaric and completely unnecessary loss of life. But it is important nonetheless to look at all of our somewhat strange and warped attitudes to the biological cycle of women without which none of us would exist. There is a wealth of study and speculation about why there remains such a taboo about even discussing menstruation. One theory is the continued shock and awe associated with women's reproductive role and capacity and the rather graphic miracle of reproduction itself. Another is the perfectly understandable fear of blood and the apparent oddness of its simultaneous association with both potential grave injury and new life. Who wants to be constantly reminded of the permanent knife-edge between life and death? Because one half of the human race does not bleed this way, that significant difference in life experience, combined with the tradition of covering it all up, probably breeds superstition and discrimination in an incredibly unhealthy way.

If the United States was the twentieth-century powerhouse behind the motorcar and the cinema, it is surely also the nation that made advertising into the multibillion-dollar trade, art form or science that it is today. In the first part of the twenty-first century, it is no longer something novel – no upstart industry – but a great receptacle of and testament to cultural and political history in what might be called the modern age. Chella Quint is a force of nature. A young clever comedian, like many of her peers before her she found that the research that went into preparing her comedic observations became something of a mission and campaign over time. 'Adventures in Menstruation' and 'Lifting the Lid' show her powers of historic and contemporary observation and wit. She uses them to demonstrate the way in which advertising in particular has been complicit in selling us sanitary products with the power of embarrassment and even shame. Quint charts the history of this branch of advertising back to the 1920s, when surplus First World War bandages were re-branded as 'sanitary towels'. Then there were the Second World War years, when women involved in the war effort needed 'protection' from the social horror of a shameful leak, followed by 1950s domestic consumerism that sealed the deal on the discreet and even attractively wrapped box that attempted to make the product and need that it was meeting 'discreet' to the point of invisibility – like too many women themselves. It is perhaps no wonder that English colloquial descriptions of menstrual periods range from being 'on' (no doubt a derivation from being 'on the rag'), to the 'time of the month' and the less euphemistic 'curse'.

More recently (and not before time), there has been a heartening feminist twist in the development of advertising for feminine hygiene products. We may trace the roots back to the positive commentary around the first appearance of an all-important shocking red, as opposed to the traditional blue dot, in a very diagrammatic Always advert in 2011. It is said to have been the brainchild of a young woman intern at the agency that held the contract. However, the loud and proud feminist hygiene advert would appear to have finally found its time with both the Always #Like a girl and Bodyform 'Blood' campaigns. The former, which began in 2014, views like an audition reel, beginning with a number of young adult women and men asked by a casting director to run, fight, throw and hit 'like a girl'. The results are cringeworthy, not least for the fact that we, the audience, are in on the feminist conspiracy from the start. Then a similar number of young girls around ten years old are asked to perform the same tasks 'like a girl'. They do so to the bravest, best and most natural of their abilities, without the same degrading stereotyping that we saw among the women in their early twenties. The older actors are then confronted with their mistake and given the opportunity to perform life's 'audition' once more. The film is punctuated by poignant music and graphics about the risks to female confidence during puberty and the manufacturer's desire to buck that trend.

The Bodyform 'Blood' advert of June 2016 is my current favourite. After nearly a century of blood avoidance in the advertising of products designed to deal with female blood, we see a beautifully cinematic commercial with plenty of it. The characters in the film are young and energetic women boxers, cross-country runners, skate-boarders, ballet dancers and even a Joan of Arc-like warrior with a sword on a horse. As happens in these occupations, the women bleed. They bleed heroically and not in embarrassment or defeat and we are left with the slogan that 'No blood should hold us back'.

I have no doubt that the work of Chella Quint and others will have influenced this extremely positive development in popular culture. Most importantly, though, she speaks warmly, humorously and honestly about an experience shared by most women the world over for about forty-odd years of their lives. She advocates that both girls and boys should be properly taught about this aspect of life before the nonsense, fear, revulsion or shame sets in. I could not agree more. A 2016 survey by Clue attracted 90,000 responses from all over the world and found slang or euphemism for periods in ten different languages as reported by 78 per cent of participants. They ranged from references to lingonberries and strawberries in Sweden and Finland respectively, to the rather hilarious if slightly antiquated French *Les Anglais ont débarqué* (The English have landed). I once heard the story of a little boy, riven with fear for his mother's life when he followed her to the toilet and found traces of blood left behind. Another boy told me that he didn't think he should have to see feminine hygiene products on display. These boys were and are the brothers, partners and fathers of the girls and women of the present and future. They need to be helped to be less afraid.

So, as always, there are the traditions and the taboos. But there is also the money. Where there is poverty, be it in the first or developed, urban or rural world, poor girls and women face an additional and significant economic hurdle. GroundUp is an extraordinary community media project working in South Africa. Here is an extract from an article by Pharie Sefali which it published in November 2014:

Akhona is in grade eight. Like many of her classmates, she often misses school when she has her periods because her family cannot afford sanitary pads. When she has to write a test, she uses a sock, she says. Sometimes by the time she gets her period her grandmother has no money left, she says.

'At home we are five children and I am the only girl who is old enough to go through periods. My grandmother is old. She sometimes forgets to buy pads and spends all the money on other household things, and it's embarrassing to ask my uncles for money to buy pads,' says Akhona. 'Sometimes if I keep on asking the neighbours for pads they don't give me because they keep on saying why don't I buy them in advance. They do not know that I do not have money for them,' says Akhona.

Her friend Noluntu, who is also in grade eight, says she missed her class test a few days ago because her period came early and no one had money to give her. The next day Akhona suggested she use a sock as a replacement until she could get a pad.

Many schoolgirls use rags, newspapers or tree bark instead of sanitary pads or tampons. UNICEF estimates that one in ten schoolgirls in Africa do not attend school while menstruating.

Noluthando Kasi, a school social worker in Langa, says many children get contraceptive injections, not because they are sexually active, but from trying to control the bleeding each month because they can't afford to buy sanitary wear. 'Some of the girls take a sock and put a little sand inside the sock so that the blood won't mess their clothing if it's a heavy flow,' says Kasi.

This report from a township of Cape Town may seem surprising and even shocking to readers in the northern hemisphere, but I can certainly remember similar desperate resort to ingenuity when some girls of my generation first had their periods in the Britain of the early 1980s. By way of reminder that we haven't come that far or have perhaps even gone backwards, the 2016 Ken Loach film *I, Daniel Blake* depicts a single mother prioritizing purchasing food for her two children and shoplifting sanitary products for herself. While some women in the US have now launched campaigns for feminine hygiene products to be provided freely like toilet paper in school, workplace and restaurant washrooms, many of its states and other countries around the world attach a sales tax of a kind usually reserved for 'luxury items'. The UK is one such country, currently with a 5 per cent sales tax applying to these products. While the Conservative government promised to abolish the tax in 2016, this pledge was quickly withdrawn in favour of taking 15 million a year from the tax in order to fund women's charities. The idea of a compulsory 'tampon tax' being used to fund women's refuges and other essential services in austerity Britain caused significant consternation. Then, to add insult to injury, it was discovered that one of the beneficiaries of this regressive tax policy was an anti-abortion counselling service.

According to the WHO in 2015, sexual and reproductive health problems constituted one third of the health issues of women between the ages of fifteen and forty-four. Unsafe sex was a major risk factor and 222 million women were not getting adequate contraception. Adolescent girls in particular are vulnerable to complications during pregnancy and childbirth, which, alongside unsafe abortions, are a leading cause of death in this age group.

Savita Halappanavar was a 31-year-old dentist, when she was admitted to hospital on 21 October 2012 complaining of pains in her back. She was seventeen weeks pregnant. Her waters broke early the next morning. When she asked whether there was any way of saving her baby, Savita was told that nothing could be done to prevent a miscarriage. The following day, on 23 October, and in the clear understanding that nothing could be done to save the unborn child, Halappanavar asked for a termination. She was told that even though miscarriage was inevitable, this was legally impossible as the monitor still displayed a foetal heartbeat. Savita went on to deliver a stillborn daughter, developed septicemia and subsequently died on 28 October. While Savita was an Indian national, these events did not take place on the subcontinent. She was living in Ireland at the time of her death at the University Hospital in Galway. The inquest found that, notwithstanding a clear diagnosis given to a qualified medical professional that her baby's fate was sealed, Halappanavar's life had not been sufficiently at risk to justify an abortion until it was too late for that procedure to have saved her life.

Amnesty International describes Ireland as having one of the most restrictive abortion law regimes in the world, alongside Andorra, Malta and San Marino, which also ban abortion, even in cases of rape, severe or even fatal foetal impairment or a risk to the woman's health. According to the Irish Central Statistics Office, there were 2,549 reported sexual offences in 2016 (the population is only 4.76 million). There is also significant under-reporting of rape. Notwithstanding substantially reformed social attitudes in recent times, including the historic referendum of May 2015 which delivered same-sex marriage to a once deeply conservative Catholic country, women's rights to reproductive autonomy and so even to life, remain at odds there with most of the developed world. An earlier constitutional referendum in 1983 secured the eighth amendment which acknowledges 'the right to life of the unborn', and crucially leaves the mother with only an 'equal right' to be weighed in the balance. This has led to a great deal of anguish and tragic results for some women, girls, their families and medical professionals.

Savita Halappanavar's death prompted much controversy and huge protests over the confusion around the application of the extremely limited abortion exemption in Irish law. This led to the passing of the Protection of Life During Pregnancy Act 2013, which creates an explicit defence to abortion where the mother's life is at 'real or substantial risk'. To abort one's foetus outside the exception is to risk fourteen years' imprisonment, notwithstanding an international human rights' consensus in favour of the decriminalization of abortion. As a result, women feel forced to travel to Great Britain, often in secret and at the personal cost involved in funding travel and accommodation and healthcare fees. Further problems and dangers arise if post-termination complications develop after these women have returned home.

In 1994, representatives from 179 countries came together at the International Conference on Population and Development. The resulting 'Programme of Action' recognized women's reproductive rights, not as a new construct, but as a necessary reflection of rights to life, dignity and autonomy that had long been established despite the considerable cultural and ethical debates around contraception and abortion. Twenty years later, the Center for Reproductive Rights (CRR) in New York charted a considerable developing consensus around making services accessible to women. The point is not to decide all ethical questions surrounding the beginning of life, but to leave more of them to the women who bear the bulk of the biological burden, including at the risk and cost of their own lives, and those of pre-existing children. The practical evidence and pragmatic case is that restrictions on abortion do not decrease its practice, but instead send it to unsafe clandestine places where women risk their health and lives. This was the rational public health policy argument long before it was taken up as a matter of personal dignity and human rights. Nonetheless in 2014, the CRR reported an average of 22 million unsafe abortions per year, 98 per cent of them in developing countries, most of which had restrictive abortion laws. These resulted in around 47,000 women's deaths and 5 million injuries from complications. The WHO estimated that nearly all of these could have been prevented by better education, family planning and the provision of safe and legal abortion and care.

By the time of the 'Programme of Action', more than a dozen African countries had liberalized abortion laws by adding or clarifying grounds for a legal termination and some had enshrined these in their constitutions. These included Burkina Faso, South Africa, Guinea, Chad, Mali,

Benin, Ethiopia, Swaziland, Niger, Togo and Kenya. There was a similar trend in Asia with liberalization in Cambodia, Nepal, Bhutan, Iran, Fiji and Indonesia.

The majority of European countries also already permitted abortion without restriction as to reason or on economic grounds. While a number of countries have further liberalized since then, the CRR observes a trend towards more restricted access in others. These include the Russian Federation, Latvia, the Slovak Republic, Germany, Macedonia and Belarus. Russia is a particular concern – no doubt on account of its size and influence. Since 2003 it has restricted the grounds for lawful abortion, culminating in a 2012 ban on abortion between weeks twelve and twenty-two of a pregnancy save in the case of rape. The state has further acted to require anti-abortion counselling, waiting periods and conscience waivers for doctors. In 2013, it banned all advertising of abortions.

In Latin America and the Caribbean, five countries are observed to have liberalized (Guyana, Saint Lucia, Colombia, Bolivia and Peru), but El Salvador legislated in 1998 to ban all abortion (previously allowed to save a woman's life or in cases of rape and foetal impairment) and Nicaragua banned all exceptions to its prohibitions in 2006.

Monitoring the position in Australia, Mexico and the United States is more complex on account of their highly federated systems. The CRR charted liberalization in four Australian states (Western Australia, Australian Capital Territory, Victoria and Tasmania), but in both Mexico and the United States it anticipates a tussle between liberalization and legal and practical restriction between the federal and state levels.

Abortion will no doubt always be a difficult subject, with or without concerns relating to religion, population growth or a host of medical advances allowing for both more effective contraception and earlier, safer and even non-hospital-based forms of termination. I have never met a woman who was 'happy' about the termination of a pregnancy as opposed to believing it to be a choice that was hers to make in difficult circumstances – as long as the choice was truly hers. So it is frustrating to say the least, when so many of those who position themselves with the so-called 'pro-life' argument also rail against early, realistic and non-judgemental sex education, the advocacy and provision of contraception and greater female autonomy in general. No one can be happy with women drinking bleach or hurting themselves with sharp objects in an attempt at a DIY termination instead of safe treatment. Surely no one wants a woman to have to contemplate suicide rather than complete her term, or die like Savita Halappanavar due to complications that could have been anticipated and prevented. To end a pregnancy will be an easier or more difficult decision, subject to a woman's medical and social circumstances. The real question for society is who should decide.

Even a wanted pregnancy can still lead to considerable risks for women in many parts of the world. Sure enough, there were huge improvements in pregnancy and childbirth care in the twentieth century, but these have yet to reach far too many women. In 2013 the estimated numbers of women who died of complications in pregnancy or labour ranged from 289,000 to 350,000. Most of these are thought to have been preventable with better facilities and care. The Fifth of the Millennium Development Goals set at UN level was to cut the maternal mortality ratio by 75 per cent globally. The fact that this was far from achieved was highlighted by Ban Ki Moon in the foreword to the Millennium Development Goals Report at the end of the monitored period in 2015.

The ratio has declined by only 45 per cent globally since 1990 (64 per cent in Southern Asia and 49 per cent in sub-Saharan Africa). Most of the reduction has occurred since the goal was set in 2000. Nonetheless, in 2013, there were still 210 dead women for every 100,000 live births in the world.

More positively, 71 per cent of births were attended by skilled health workers in 2014. This was up from 59 per cent in 1990. In Northern Africa, the number of women in receipt of four or more antenatal visits increased from 50 per cent to 89 per cent between 1990 and 2014.

Amnesty International has voiced particular concern about maternal mortality among rural women in Peru (despite it being a middle-income country), Burkina Faso and Sierra Leone. More surprising perhaps, is the maternal healthcare crisis in the USA as observed by Amnesty as late as 2010. Despite the USA spending more on healthcare than any other country and more on maternity than other hospital care, Amnesty described US women as having a higher risk of dying of pregnancy-related complications than those in forty-nine other countries, including Kuwait, Bulgaria and South Korea. Rather shockingly, African-American women were nearly four times as likely to die of complications in pregnancy than white women and that comparison had not improved for over twenty years in a healthcare system riven with inequality, discrimination and financial and other barriers to adequate care. Year after year, the US remains one of the wealthiest nations on the planet.

So, steady improvement notwithstanding, the state of global maternal health remains a depressing one, not least because it is a story not of inadequate science or lack of resources but ultimately of a lack of priority, and political and economic will. When the UN's eight Millennium Development Goals of 2000 were replaced by the seventeen Sustainable

Development Goals of 2016, there were goals on both 'good health and well-being' and 'gender equality', but no longer a stand-alone goal of 'improving maternal health'.

It may lack the drama of maternal mortality, but mental health conditions are a significant problem in pregnancy and after childbirth. The WHO estimates that 13 per cent of women suffer some kind of disorder – often depression – after childbirth, with this rising to around 20 per cent in developing countries. Even in the twenty-first century and even among women, matters relating to mental health remain too strong a taboo to be tackled with the care and resources that they need and deserve. Women the world over describe symptoms ranging from anxiety around parental responsibility and even positive fear of the infant to a sense of 'not really being there' to profound depression and thoughts of suicide. One woman to whom I promised anonymity said this:

The pregnancy had gone well enough but the birth was difficult and even a little dangerous. When I came home I was emotionally and physically exhausted and I did not have very much support. Feelings of exhaustion soon turned into those of inadequacy and fear when I realized that this tiny creature was so dependent on me and would be – it seemed – for ever. I didn't really talk to anyone about this until years later. It didn't seem right. It was supposed to be such a moment of joy. Family, friends, neighbours and even relative strangers had flocked, often uninvited, to the hospital ward and then my home. They were there to see the baby of course – not me. There were moments when I felt completely worthless like I had served my purpose and was now washed up. I felt so alone and cried a lot, but it all seemed to pass with time.

But for other women these feelings are both worse and harder to escape without some kind of therapeutic or clinical intervention.

Menopause is yet another moment in female development that is too little discussed and is fraught with both physical and psychological challenges that too many women must face with insufficient medical, social and emotional support. We aren't taught about it in school, our mothers maintain the conspiracy of silence and even female friends and colleagues, who could make such a difference with their shared experience, understanding and empathy, are slow to talk about this completely natural transition in a woman's life. There is so much discussion, debate, advice and solidarity around reproduction itself. Why may not some of the same energy, advice and adjustment be offered to women who have themselves so much still to offer?

These are not the only times when women's mental health can come under strain. It is thought that throughout life, they are more likely than men to experience anxiety, depression and physical symptoms that seem not to have an obvious medical explanation. Depression is the most common mental health problem for women and suicide is a leading cause of death in women under sixty. Unsurprisingly, women who have been exposed to violence at the hands of intimate partners are twice as likely to have problems with depression and alcohol and four times more likely to commit suicide. This is just one of the many ways in which the social position, as opposed to the biological condition of women, is thought to play a major role in the state of their mental health. From problems with body image and anorexia in adolescence and beyond, to the depression related to not being the perfect wife, mother, worker and even grandmother later on, every aspect of social pressure and inequality brings a challenge to

97

health and happiness. This is further complicated by the expectations which we all have about what is or is not 'normal' and 'healthy' male and female behaviour.

The clear consensus is that mental health issues and services have been neglected the world over for far too long. A lack of funding, priority and mainstreaming has been compounded by centuries of stigma attached to both men and women who struggle to cope with the various practical and psychological pressures of survival and loss, however average or extreme. The flip-side of this enormous challenge is the equivalent opportunity to make things better, not just for individual people, but families, communities, societies and even the world. I asked a veteran mental health professional – one of the wisest people I know – what her prescription for better mental health would look like. Of course she talked about the public spending required to fund various treatments for those in need who otherwise suffer in silence or linger on waiting lists that deliver too little too late. Yet it was when I offered her the free hand and the magic wand that the conversation really became interesting. She spoke positively and excitedly of the greater number of men who would now actively seek help compared to when she began her career many decades ago. She talked of the inspiration that can come from group counselling – perhaps chosen for reasons of cost but nonetheless hugely beneficial in easing isolation and teaching people to listen to and communicate with each other and themselves. The thought of women and men, boys and girls getting access to therapeutic services even outside moments of crisis may seem like a pipe dream. However, when this is balanced against the cost of decreased labour participation and chronic non-communicable illnesses (such as obesity and substance and alcohol abuse) that are linked with depression, the sums make so much sense.

Accessible counselling in every community, workplace and educational institution, combined with an increased focus on mental health in the provision of medical services, could make a world of difference to all of our lives at least at some stage.

Which brings me back to the good doctor's prescription of power as the best treatment for women's ill-health. Whether physical, mental, reproductive or more general, no substantial and sustained global improvements in women's health outcomes can be achieved without improving their finance and freedom and the circumstances governing every other aspect of life. As women come to matter more and gain greater power and priority for the things that matter to them, they will be better placed to take care of their bodies, diets, physical safety and psychological needs. The benefits to families, communities and wider societies could be immeasurable if we return to the 1948 aspiration of physical, mental and social well-being.

5. Home

What does the idea of 'home' mean to you? If you close your eyes and say the word, does it invoke a feeling or an image? Do you hear cars, cows or chatter, church bells or a call to prayer in the distance? Perhaps you remember the distinctive good (or bad) taste of a particular food, or even the smell of herbs, spices, flowers or soap.

I have heard so many women and men, boys and girls, describe the notion of home in different ways. It inspires hundreds of thousands of poems, songs, stories and dramas across the ages and the world. It can be something to plan, live, fight and even die for, or something permanently to yearn for and regret living without. Yet it invariably involves some combination of a personally special place and/or people that creates some sense of safety and belonging. It can relate to country, community, bricks and mortar or loved ones, in various combinations and to different degrees. It can be something reasonably or hopefully permanent, or increasingly commonly perhaps, something that evolves and ideally improves, over a lifetime.

I have spoken before about my parents' concept of 'home' when I was a child in the 1970s and 80s. Having migrated from India to London some years before, they worked hard to achieve what some people have come to describe as 'a place on the housing ladder', but they always thought of it as their semi-detached home. Children were not allowed in their previous rented bedsitter, and like so many people they also aspired to tending a small garden. Hence the pressure to move when I came along in 1969. They had no extended family in the UK and trips to India were, for them at least, prohibitively expensive for many years. So instead, they filled their small house with friends from all over the world. These they warmly and generously entertained, despite their limited resources. My mother was that kind of miracle cook, always ready for the extra or unexpected guest, and I suppose rice-based meals can lend themselves to that. As long as you have enough rice, that is. In what was no doubt an insecurity based on her own youth, I rarely saw her more worried than when the family-sized plastic dustbin under the stairs (specially scrubbed for a novel purpose) was less than half full of rice. What I sometimes lacked in blood relatives, 'mother tongues' and traditions, I gained in cross-generational family friends. They brought their food and stories from many countries. It may have taken me the best part of forty years, but at least I now realize what a huge gift and influence this was for me.

Nonetheless, my parents did periodically talk of another 'home'. This was the place of their birth, to which they hoped perhaps to return one day. This left me confused when it should not have done. I think perhaps I almost resented them having another version of home in which I did not feature. I was born in London and at that point had no non-English language skills whatsoever. This was of course completely unfair and even more than a little narcissistic of me, given that I, like most children of my generation in Britain, aspired to 'flying the nest' in order to make a new and independent home of my own one day. In my defence, I had been small in a period of rising racism and anti-migrant feeling (sound familiar?), and even senior Conservative politicians suggested that the loyalty of people like my parents should be subjected to some kind of 'cricket test', whereby

Commonwealth migrants might be deemed suspect for cheering on any other national team in a Test match against England. I didn't want my family inadvertently to play into such hands. Looking back, I was far too defensive. Even with a certain inevitable nostalgia, in their adventures in food, friendship and every aspect of British and European culture, my parents were true Londoners long before I was. Many years later, I asked my mother – still in the warmth of her much-cherished 'semi' – if she retained hopes of retiring to the land of her childhood one day. She shook her head and replied, 'Home is where your children are.'

Sadly, this is far from the practical or emotional reality, or even remotest option, for far too many people in the world today. Firstly, there are well over 65 million displaced persons. Then there are probably over 1.6 billion homeless or in inadequate housing, and incalculable numbers of people emotionally displaced or disconnected from friends and loved ones. Surely, the sheer scale of this economic, social and emotional misery is wholly unnecessary in the first quarter of the twenty-first century.

Article 25 (1) of the 1948 Universal Declaration of Human Rights states:

> Everyone has the right to a standard of living adequate for the health and well-being of himself and his family, including food, clothing, housing and medical care and necessary social services, and the right to security in the event of unemployment, sickness, disability, widowhood, old age or other lack of livelihood in circumstances beyond his control.

This is in turn reflected in article 11 (1) of the 1966 International Covenant on Economic, Social and Cultural Rights:

The State Parties to the present Covenant recognize the right of everyone to an adequate standard of living for himself and his family, including adequate food, clothing and housing, and to the continuous improvement of living conditions. The State Parties will take appropriate steps to ensure the realization of this right, recognizing to this effect the essential importance of international co-operation based on free consent.

A number of UN committees and General Assembly statements have emphasized the concept of 'adequacy' as the right to live somewhere in 'security, peace and dignity'. This has been further explained as including a number of individual practical elements. One crucial component of a secure home would appear to be some form of legal security of tenure or protection from eviction. Another would be the availability of necessary services and other aspects of location (such as the ability to access work). Reasonable affordability is clearly crucial if adequate shelter is to be a fundamental right and not a mere privilege. Habitability should involve things like decent basic infrastructure, privacy, space, physical security, lighting and ventilation. For disadvantaged groups (such as the disabled) in particular, the accessibility of any dwelling can be a matter of vital importance. Further, there can be important cultural concerns. For some people 'home' must be a place where family and even extended family members of different generations can live either together or in close proximity. Yet for others, that kind of arrangement would be the last thing to aspire to, and perhaps rather something to escape. All in all, our international human rights framework seems to provide a perfectly sensible, sensitive and universal understanding of the kind of shelter in which anyone might begin to build or foster a sense of 'home'.

Sceptics from the right of the political spectrum will always seek to diminish the viability or importance of social and economic rights, just as some from the left have at times considered civil and political liberties somehow too individualistic or even bourgeois. Each brand of doubter sees some or all of these freedoms as the business purely of pragmatic politics, rather than of law or principle. Both are mistaken and, in my view, most self-evidently so in the context of the private sphere of the home. Civil and political rights, for example, to respect for personal privacy or family life, and even basic human security, are extremely hard, perhaps impossible, to realize without adequate shelter. The converse is equally true. What kind of social right to adequate housing would not guarantee an element of privacy, security or the ability to live with the family or loved ones of one's choosing? The reason why these fundamental rights are indivisible is because they provide for the whole human being and everything that she needs to live and thrive.

The home is an ideal testing ground for my proposition. Who today would dream of calling family or friends to the dinner table with the edict that they may choose to share the meal, or the conversation, but not both (one right being defined as of a socio-economic nature and the other of a civil and political one)? Would you invite a guest to stay the night on the sofa or in a vacant room, but only if they agreed to go to the bathroom with the door open or to be monitored by a camera while they slept? Of course you would not inflict such an indignity in the safe space of your home. You surely consider it, at least in part, your duty to protect people under your care or hospitality. At a societal level, some of this duty must be discharged at state level, not least when there is so much homelessness and inadequate shelter and when people are exposed to violence and other dangers in dwellings that more resemble prison than any notion of home. Of course some rights and freedoms (such as free speech) must ultimately be guaranteed by law and judges and others (such as adequate food and housing) by politics and economics. However, all of these rights are essential for everyone, and their effective delivery invariably requires the support and investment of a number of state and non-state participants alike.

It is therefore especially alarming that in March 2017, the UN Special Rapporteur on the Right to Housing, Leilani Farha, felt compelled to make the following remarks to the UN Human Rights Council:

> Housing has lost its social function and is seen instead as a vehicle for wealth and asset growth. It has become a financial commodity, robbed of its connection to community, dignity and the idea of home.

Describing this state of affairs as 'an issue of accountability', she went on to say:

> The consequences of placing the interests of investors before human rights are stark. Millions of people around the world are being evicted through foreclosures, or being displaced by development and priced out of cities.

Coming around a decade after the global financial crisis fuelled by the lending policies of offering 'sub-prime' mortgages to middle- and lower-income people in an inflated housing market, Farha's words are poignant indeed. 'Properties' (sometimes multiple properties) having become assets for some, have accordingly deprived too many others of much needed shelter, or at least rendered that shelter less and less affordable and secure. Resilient though human beings are, without basic shelter it is very hard for most of us to imagine any real sense of home.

As so often, the position worldwide is worse for women. Old laws or alternatively long-held custom and practice (sometimes flying in the face of more recently established equalizing laws) too often discriminate against women's rights to housing, land, property, inheritance and security. This is not simply a question of economic disadvantage but of a greater dependence on men that inevitably leaves women even more vulnerable to violence, destitution and hunger. The position is worse still for widows, divorcees, single women or those in informal or unrecognized marriages. Too many are left without anything that you might even begin to describe as a secure home.

In 2003, Human Rights Watch reported the testimony of an anonymous Kenyan woman:

> When my husband died, his relatives came and took everything. They told me to take my clothes in a paper bag and leave. I left, because if I had resisted they would have beat me up. The relatives identified someone to inherit me. It was a cousin of my husband. They told me, 'Now you are of less value, so we'll give you to anyone available to inherit you.' I didn't say anything.

It is a haunting voice, coming as it does three years into the twenty-first century from a democracy thought to be one of the biggest and most advanced economies in East and Central Africa. Sadly, this kind of story is far from unique in Africa or indeed other places in the world. The UN Office of the High Commissioner for Human Rights suggests that there are still many customary laws and practices that assume housing, land and property to be the province of men and therefore leave widows vulnerable to their in-laws, and even to violent eviction at their hands. Daughters are also often barred from inheritance on the grounds that they will eventually marry, and so it is thought, their brothers should obviously be favoured.

The better news perhaps lies in examples of law reform in an attempt to improve the lot of widows in particular, and women in general. Sierra Leone passed a new inheritance statute in 2007 entitling spouses (under civil or customary law) and cohabiting partners to inherit. It also protects women from undue interference from extended family. Previously, the property of those (usually men) who had died without making a will would have passed to their parents and brothers. This is theoretically at least a significant protection for women and children.

The 1994 Rwandan genocide left a great many widows and consequential housing and land problems. New matrimonial law in 1999 is thought to have been important in equalizing the inheritance rights of sons and daughters and towards allowing widows to take on and control their homes. However, it may take many more years yet before we see the full implementation and acceptance of such changes. As so often, law is in danger of remaining a dead letter without significantly widespread cultural acceptance and the ability to enforce it. That involves political will, legal aid and ultimately the policing required to protect vulnerable women and their homes, whatever the technical legal entitlement. Furthermore, without cultural acceptance or at least significant social support, it is very difficult to prevent women signing any property rights away for fear of rape or murder or of being rendered a social outcast.

Then there are the blatant or more complex legal anomalies

that remain, and usually to the practical disadvantage of a woman's right to inheritance. For instance, Article 23 of the Zambian Constitution guarantees non-discrimination in law and its application, including on the basis of sex, but then makes an exception for laws relating to adoption, marriage, divorce and the distribution of property after death (i.e. so many of the laws especially important to any attempt at improving women's rights and independence).

The Constitution of Botswana makes explicit recognition of gender equality, but this is at odds with customary law, which discriminates against women in matters such as property and inheritance. In practice therefore, women are once more in jeopardy of losing their homes on the death of their husbands. Similarly in Uganda, where both the Constitution and the Land Act outlaw discrimination against women and protect widows and children, there is conflict with entrenched customary law that women do not own land. Even inheritance law, which grants the widows of intestate men 15 per cent of the property, is said to be practically unenforceable against the opposing interests of the husband's other relatives.

Similar discrimination endures in North Africa and the Middle East as a result of both customary and statute law, much of which is based on certain interpretations of Islam that grant lesser shares of any inheritance to women than would apply to the equivalent man. Even in secular Turkey, where the law provides for equal inheritance rights, there is considerable pressure on women to renounce any claims, or face social exclusion, harassment, threats and violence. Such extra-legal resistance to women's inheritance is also said to be a feature in Morocco (notwithstanding the adoption of a non-discriminatory Family Code in 2004) and in Jordan.

As discussed earlier, the best-intended equalizing inheritance laws can be circumvented by either a man leaving his property to his sons rather than his wife in his lifetime, or a woman being pressured to renounce her share in any property to relatives after his death. In 2011, the head of the Sharia High Court of the Occupied Palestinian Territory attempted to deal with the latter problem by imposing certain conditions on any renunciation of inheritance. These include a four-month period after the death, before which no such renunciation can be registered, and a report by independent experts as to the true value of the property. Importantly, increasing numbers of Islamic thinkers now openly state their view that there is nothing in the original teachings of Islam to prevent equality for men and women in matters of inheritance.

Insecurity on inheritance is just one of the reasons why too many women and men in the world are vulnerable to eviction. While such action cannot be ruled out entirely (e.g. in the cases of persistent non-payment of rent, damage to property or harm to other tenants), it should be an absolute last resort. Further, there is a big difference between an eviction that complies with international law and the experience of so many. No one should be rendered homeless. Nor should they be evicted without consultation and adequate notice, nor without access to legal advice and redress. Neutral state officials (e.g. police officers) should be present and able to identify themselves properly. Eviction should not happen in bad weather or at night. Forced eviction is obviously traumatic for anyone, but in most parts of the world women's experience of it is especially bad. They are likely to be more vulnerable to violence, including rape. They may have lost, not only a home, but a place where they were engaging in some kind of commercial home-working activity. They are most likely to be homeless with the care of children, and are at particular risk on the street.

State officials could also themselves become the abusive perpetrators of forced eviction rather than acting as the victims' protective witnesses (let alone guardians) as they should. In recent decades in both Myanmar and Indonesia, thousands of women have been targeted for rape and other forms of brutality by military and other state agents during eviction and relocation.

Natural disasters and climate change also take a dispro-portionate toll on women. This has been evident in the early part of this century at the time of the Indian Ocean tsunami of 2004, the South Asia and Haiti earthquakes of 2005 and 2010, and Hurricane Katrina in 2005. Women were (and are) more likely to be living in the most inadequate and vulner-able housing to begin with and are then more susceptible to violence and abuse in temporary shelter or if homeless. It is for other books and writers to evidence and articulate the relationship between man-made destruction of the environ-ment and so-called 'natural disasters'. What I must observe, however, is the role of power and property versus poverty in people's and especially women's vulnerability to them, and in the context of post-disaster reconstruction. After Hurri-cane Katrina devastated New Orleans, the UN reported how the United States' reconstruction efforts prioritized owner-occupiers rather than the rental sector. Notwith-standing that before the winds came, half the population of the city were tenants. Women were the 'heads' of 77 per cent of the publicly owned households before the disaster and 88 per cent of those relying on public financial support for their rent. According to the Brookings Institution and the London School of Economics report 'A Year of Living Dangerously: A Review of Natural Disasters in 2010', they inevitably suffered the most from the lack of affordable housing after the hurricane.

Then, in June 2017, in one of the wealthiest boroughs of one of the wealthiest cities in the world, at least eighty people died in a preventable disaster that will for ever be associated with austerity, deregulation and the cost- and corner-cutting that are too often permissible when it comes to protecting the lives of the poor. Grenfell Tower was a social housing tower block of 129 flats owned by Kensington and Chelsea London Borough Council when a fire burned out of control for twenty-four hours, and was only finally extinguished after sixty. At the time of writing a public inquiry is pending but significant concerns have been extensively aired as to the adequacy of building materials, maintenance and fire regulations. In an interview with the *Guardian* newspaper, my friend, colleague and Shadow Foreign Secretary Emily Thornberry MP said this of the lessons to be learned from the Grenfell disaster:

> We are not a developing country, we're a developed country – and a tower can burn down, all those people lose their lives, and if that were not bad enough, the aftermath . . . the idea that you come out in your knickers, you have nothing, and all you can do is hope there is a church nearby and someone will have donated a mattress to sleep on. What happened to the welfare state? What happened to the idea that we were all safe, because we looked after each other in Britain, we looked out for each other?

I must return to the United States, for a reminder of how the financial crisis born of the sub-prime mortgage scandal inflicted its own devastation on the right to adequate housing in so many parts of the world. Women were already at the bottom of the pile when it came to financial security before this disaster built on political short-sightedness and financial speculation and greed. They were and remain among the groups most likely to be vulnerable to predatory lending and more likely to face foreclosure and homelessness as a consequence. Then the bitterest of pills, as the economic recession that followed brought yet more unfair, discriminatory and counterproductive results. A number of wealthier countries, including the US itself, have cut both domestic social and housing programmes and vital foreign development aid. This seems to me as desperately illogical as punishing the victims of crime or trying to stay warm by burning down the house.

Yet, vital though effective economic, legal, land and housing policies are, they are not the whole story as far as 'home' or the most personal sphere is concerned. Of course there is both the natural and man-made universe of the physical world and how its resources are shared and societies constructed and governed. However, as human beings, it is also our lot to explore and inhabit the inner universe of our minds. Sometimes I think this may be an even more challenging 'final frontier' than the outer space explored by so many real and fictional heroes of recent decades. As social creatures, how we feel about ourselves inevitably affects the lives of others, and this is never more true than in the case of those with whom we share our closest relationships.

It is hard to believe that we are rapidly approaching the fiftieth anniversary of the publication of Germaine Greer's *The Female Eunuch* in 1970. This book rocked the world. It is still read and re-read, offering so many insights to generations of women and, I have no doubt, many men as well. Greer has subsequently been the first to admit that much has changed (both for the better and for the worse) since she wrote this seminal twentieth-century feminist tract. In later editions and other writing, she acknowledges the importance of the fall of the Soviet Bloc in extending consumerism and diminishing social care for a great number of women. She appreciates why the advent of HIV/AIDS has rightly caused a necessary rethink around 1960s ideas of sex without question or commitment. In 1990, she wrote in a foreword to a new anniversary edition:

> Twenty years ago it was important to stress the right to sexual expression and far less important to underline a woman's right to reject male advances . . . The argument . . . is still valid, none the less, for it holds that a woman has the right to express her own sexuality which is not at all the same thing as the right to capitulate to male advances.

Educational, entertaining and enlightening though they invariably are, a few of her more scholarly treatments of history, literature and culture may not be for everyone outside the academy, and some aspects of the discussion of a first world woman's life, work and apparently rather limited play, do perhaps seem a little of their time today. However (and I have discussed this with readers significantly younger than me), other chapters and passages are as devastatingly fresh, insightful and creative now as they must have seemed in 1970. To my mind at least, this is rarely more the case than when Germaine Greer – at the time only around thirty years old – speaks plainly from her own experience and in her own audaciously authentic voice, relatively unpeppered by the wise words of others. It is never more true than when she urges women to do as she has clearly done and to liberate their own thinking. This is most important perhaps in her discussions of 'family', healthy intimate relationships and a good life. Much of this thinking is to be found in the final third section of her classic work, bravely and simply entitled: 'Love'.

I cannot here do justice to the full sweep of Greer's cultural foundations from the classical period to the Western world of the so-called 'Swinging Sixties'. Instead I propose shamelessly to extract words and thoughts of timeless inspiration and to reflect on their potential application to our current moment. Early on in her critique of 'the Ideal' of romantic love, she cuts through the romance to make the most practical observation of the impossibility of love between a superior and an inferior:

> The proper subject for love is one's equal, seeing as the essence of love is to be mutual, and the lesser cannot produce anything greater than itself.

There is lengthy argument to back up this assertion, from the perspective of both the financially, socially and emotionally insecure woman and the man with whom she is almost compelled by society and circumstance to be in a relationship. How could one possibly disagree? No doubt a mischievous traditionalist might argue that neither the love that a parent has for a child, nor that which God is said to have for all of us, can be based on equality. Children, though, are people in the earliest stages of physical, intellectual and emotional development, and the relational inequality between them and their parents must surely even out over time. This must be especially true with people living longer in so many parts of the world and with so many adult children (most often women) therefore taking on caring responsibilities for physically and mentally frail older family members. Further, the age-old comparison of women with children (though relevant to disempowerment and even slave labour) is hardly the most attractive argument in the twenty-first century against striving for greater equality within intimacy. As for God, if he, she or they and therefore divine love truly exists, it is surely not comparable with anything that mere mortals can offer or understand, whether in marriage or any other similar relationships.

I have to agree with Greer that it is hard to conceive of a happy and healthy intimate relationship – in or outside of marriage or cohabitation between people of whatever sex or sexuality – that does not have a certain overall sense of equality about it. I do not mean precise formal equality down to every single penny of the finances or every aspect of work, talent or skill. Some people seem more than happy to rub along together perfectly well with arrangements for domestic tasks and outside work and interests that complement their shared lives. This 'sharing' is wonderful when real and not in truth (whether deliberately or not) illusory and exploitative, and as long as the relationship does not substitute for each person's practical and material independence, aspiration and sense of self. I know that it can be fashionably romantic to applaud the long marriage that ended in the death of one partner, swiftly to be followed by the 'pining', demise and death of the other. But is there not something more life-affirming to be observed of the surviving partner of however long, close, happy and reciprocal a relationship, who has sufficient financial, emotional and practical resources and skills to go on, live still and live well? This person, of whatever sex, must have somehow retained enough of their inner self to adapt to a new stage and situation. Subject to their age, health and ability, they might shop and cook a little, deal with personal administration of whatever kind, and most importantly perhaps, make friends and be in the world.

Never is the danger greater of marital or other partnership relationships, however initially mutual, becoming increasingly less equal than when children are added to the equation. Sure enough, there are no doubt many more working women, including in more high-prestige and better remunerated jobs and professions than there were in 1970, but the arrival of children brings great change, regardless of geography, class and generation, when a woman is facing choices about what she wants and can afford to do, from both financial and emotional perspectives.

In a now famous sequence from her chapter called 'Family', the young Germaine Greer describes an ideal or aspiration, or perhaps it was only a musing or pipe dream that she once had, of a new do-it-yourself version of the rural extended family. It was her brave, honest and best attempt to balance her own embryonic desires and ambitions with her understanding of the needs of others. Her work was mostly in cities, and she believed that children should enjoy the delights of country life, and indeed of the company of other children, as in traditional extended families. She imagined a house in Italy, acquired and shared by a group of friends, perhaps in collaboration with a local family. The children and perhaps some of the adults would spend long periods there while others would come from other countries and cities as work and time allowed. She admitted that she had no 'blueprint', and provided no detail about financial, legal and other crucial obligations which, when left unclear, can often lead to conflict. Perhaps relatively few people in the world have consciously or otherwise pursued such an experiment in the decades since. It is ripe for pastiche and even attack as either a flawed hippy dream or an extended middle-class Tuscan holiday. Yet there may be some inspiration to be taken from it nonetheless.

Let us be clear that the close or proximately living extended family is often sentimentalized as some kind of idyll, even though so many people spend their lives trying to escape its surveillance, judgement and control. The question is whether it might be possible to achieve the support that may be associated with the best of the extended family, without its more oppressive qualities. That seems to be what Greer was craving though, unlike me, I think she was sceptical of the state's ability to facilitate or support this kind of balance between community and autonomy, support and freedom. Striving towards this balance is vital, not as some utopia (for those who can readily afford or aspire to something like the privately owned shared house in the country), but as a practical approach to enhancing the life chances of everyone, everywhere, young and old. We are social creatures and mostly need and want to live together in either families and/or communities of whatever increasingly variable shape and size. Yet surely no one should be controlled or enslaved in the process. That is the bedrock of post-war human rights thinking. If it can be embraced and applied (at least in theory and by some) at international and state level, why not in the more local or intimate context of community and home?

Notions of intergenerational community or even 'family' have not always been about blood. Those of us who were raised and conditioned to 'fall in love' and marry or cohabit go on to 'join' something other than our birth family. This is especially true in societies where consanguinity or marriage between first cousins, is frowned upon or forbidden. Thus we are used to developing some of the strongest ties in life with a person and people who begin as relative strangers to us. There is a famous and perhaps even over-used Nigerian (Igbo and Yoruba) adage that says 'it takes a whole village to raise a child'. There are in fact many similar proverbs in different languages from around the African continent: 'one knee does not bring up a child' (Sukuma); 'one hand does not nurse a child' (Swahili). The strength of this tradition is no doubt just as well given the number of HIV/AIDS orphans in need of informal adoption and fostering in recent decades. Then there are the orphans and refugees of conflict and natural disasters all over the world, and the informal 'reverse' adoption and fostering of older people by the young in migrant and displaced communities missing the extended families of their past.

Many people in modern and increasingly mobile and fluid city life seize the opportunity of building strong ties with friends, colleagues or those with whom they share an interest in sport, culture, religion, politics or other pastimes. Some of these ties and relationships may even become greater and more supportive than those of a traditional family, which may for many be increasingly disparate or far away. We must also take into account the complex nature of modern families, nowadays sometimes shaped as much by divorce or the desire to stay single or childless, as by marriage and cohabitation. Single and step-parents, half-siblings and tight friendship circles celebrate the good times and rally in the bad ones, as traditional families might once have done. A more socially liberal and non-judgemental society is ultimately, I believe, a positive thing for women, men and children, but only if this new freedom comes complete with an equivalent sense of social responsibility, capable of extending well beyond the bounds of the traditional family of whatever size.

With growing ageing populations, a number of people in the first world are beginning to think about ways of shared and community living with which to approach the later stages of their lives. But why need we wait until then? Why might we not recognize the potential benefits of intergenerational community living and support much earlier on? Why should housing, schooling, childcare and social care not be designed and located more proximately and with that in mind? Why so often in urban or suburban sprawls are there rows upon rows of houses, without a community centre, crèche, library or other shared space or social amenity in sight? Offering universal pre-school childcare could lift the life chances of millions of women and children, worldwide. Breakfast and after-school clubs have benefited poorer children's nutrition, education and life chances in both the first and developing worlds. They help mothers' ability to enter and stay in the workplace and improve the adequacy of children's care and supervision. They can also provide more professionally and personally rewarding work for properly trained women and men, and ease the isolation of mothers and children alike.

Many increasingly seem to fear or predict that automation will inevitably put millions, maybe billions, of people out of work and wealth. Why should that necessarily be the case? Why can we not learn to value each other more? Why not harness automation to the greater good, while investing in people's living standards, well-being and more paid work in caring for others?

Automation has already helped generations of women in many parts of the world. Televisions, computers, refrigerators, cookers and washing machines have long since entertained the children, preserved and cooked the food, and laundered the family's clothes. Grandparents now read their grandchildren bedtime stories via 'FaceTime' from hundreds or thousands of miles away, while Mum or Dad makes supper. This is a wonderful example of the light rather than the dark side of 'the Force' that is the internet. Long may all of this continue and develop. But why should it not be accompanied and supplemented by the grandchild-less older people next door, who might either volunteer or be paid to do the same in person, especially perhaps for children without living grandparents of their own? Further, with so many women and men working shifts and especially in low-paid work, quality round-the-clock childcare is an all-too-scarce and expensive commodity in many places where traditional family and community ties are no longer as strong as they once were. Of course, if everyone were guaranteed a basic living income, voluntarism would be something far more genuinely voluntary, democratic and non-exploitative.

Such an income guarantee could also go some way to empowering women and men who work exclusively in the home out of choice, or at least for the early part of their children's, or the later part of their parents' or other relatives' or friends' lives. It could give people the opportunity to study and/or retrain at various stages of hopefully longer and more fulfilled lives. If this kind of policy were combined with more decent social, regulated and crucially affordable housing, no one need feel trapped into either premature or over-long unequal and unhappy intimate relationships, and certainly not abusive ones.

Which brings me to another important timeless feminist proposition: that of the perils of insularity, atomization and isolation in the context of either obsessive romantic love, or the too closed, co-dependent and inward-looking, ticking 'nuclear' family of the modern age. Greer discusses this in very many contexts, and with a number of arguments as to its grave dangers for all the men, women and children concerned. One of the most profound and compelling is her understanding of the inherent insecurity of life, against which we can never really insure or insulate, and which we would do well to learn to live with in as positive and healthy a way as possible. This chapter is Greer at her eloquent best. It is a short and incisive nugget, even for those with insufficient time to read the whole book. I will not attempt to cite or summarize it, but instead offer a small take of my own.

Life can be wonderful. It can be full of joy and excitement as well as loss and sadness. We all do our best to protect ourselves, loved ones, communities and countries from unnecessary risk and danger. Yet some risk and danger are an inevitable part of life – as is death. Attempts at the risk-free life are not only futile, but in danger of imprisoning us all. This is well evidenced under totalitarian regimes, but also in markedly unequal, unhappy and abusive homes. These are of course extreme examples, deliberately selected to make the point. In all the space in between them, at both the macro and micro levels, however, are a host of individual life choices and experiences limited by fear. I am sure you can recall many examples from people, and perhaps (but not necessarily) especially women, you might know or have known. That selfless friend, neighbour, family member or co-worker who never seemed to do anything except for others. They were always working in the workplace or in the home. They lived a blameless life that was nonetheless so unfairly taken, or blighted by tragedy of whatever kind.

I believe in a world and society where people should be as reasonably protected as possible from threats of the financial, elemental, violent and health-related kinds. This takes greater equality and investment. That in turn requires a greater solidarity and a sense of community between people at the local, regional, national and international levels. But I also believe in preparing people for the almost inevitable circumstance of some protections proving imperfect or impossible. However, this even greater ambition takes investment as well.

So many people are taught, right from the cradle, always to be 'good girls and boys', with all the gendered differences in those two related sets of instructions. Know your place (however humble or exalted). Be good and work hard at home and at school. Then do your bit as a young adult (subject to your sex and circumstances). Work. Fit in. Marry. Have children. Look after them for ever. Carry on working or not (once more subject to your sex and circumstances). Do what is required to fit in with the neighbours and/or wider family. Look after any dwelling that you are fortunate enough to occupy or possess. Feed the family. If things are going reasonably well, look forward to whatever treats you look forward to (again subject to circumstances). These may be a host of guilty or public pleasures such as food, drink, entertainment, sport, seeing friends or family, holidays and so on. You are the hard-working human after all. Work. Work for retirement and look forward to it. You do your best and ask for little. And yet, and yet, unemployment, accident, illness, disability, estrangement, bereavement and death still come, and not always as anticipated or scheduled.

I do not mean to make you miserable and do not feel that way myself. Learning to rationalize and deal with insecurity can be its own freedom. It might also encourage us to stand up and question the status quo now and then. Mostly, I would wish for people to have the emotional as well as the financial resources to prepare for the unexpected, just as it seems a prodigious Germaine Greer did, nearly my whole lifetime ago. In my opinion at least, this would take investment in social and economic infrastructure. You cannot eat positive thinking or live in it. But it would also require a different approach to emotional health, in society, in healthcare, the home and in our innermost selves. The common thread between all of these elements is care for the self of course, but also a reciprocal care and concern for all other people. In the wider sphere, this can be referred to as society, solidarity, community or fellowship. In the more private realm, we tend to talk of family, friendship and love. All of these concepts have been written about at length by people far better qualified than I. They have different sounds, colours and poetry. But for me at least, they are all but aspects of the same overwhelming human instinct. We are ultimately social creatures, and achieve our best lives and potential in solidarity with others. Intimate solidarity equals love.

6. School

And now for some good news. I am able to write this provocation, as you are to read, critique, take it or leave it as you see fit. With all the enormous problems in the world today for everyone, not least women and girls, let's never make the mistake of forgetting to celebrate and build upon the most important recent success in finding and sharing the keys to our kingdom – education.

As with most stories, the seeds of this plot are sown, however humbly, very early on. I cannot remember a life or even a room without the presence of books. My earliest memories are of my mother reading to me. There were fairy tales, fables and nursery rhymes of course, but I am glad to say that alongside Cinderella and Sleeping Beauty were the Ladybird lives of real women from history, such as pioneering scientist Marie Curie and Queen Victoria. I can remember my first morning at 'school'. It was actually only the nursery class of what was to be my primary school and I had already attended a play group for at least a year. But this was the day that somehow felt special. I had a blue satchel with orange piping and my mother wrote my name inside it. There was more reading, named coat-pegs and a free daily carton of milk for each of us, distributed by whoever was the proud 'monitor' chosen for that week. After the first year of mornings only came the huge excitement of a full school day, complete with a nutritious meal at lunchtime. For I must confess that I am older even than the fast food that became the staple of too many schools later on. This was the beginning of the gift that still keeps on giving, the blessing of my free and precious British state education. It ended seventeen years later with the completion of a three-year law degree. During those last years, I was further supported by the state with a maintenance grant that went a very long way towards food, rent and books. No tuition fees or inevitable crippling loan for my generation of students in England. Only a social and moral debt that in my view we have yet completely to repay.

The benefits of education to every aspect of a happy, healthy and rewarding human life cannot be overstated. Nor can the particular benefits especially to girls and women, their own children and wider communities. It is said that infant mortality is halved when the mothers in question are literate. Some have also calculated that a woman's lifetime income can be increased by as much as 15 per cent for each extra year she spends in education. Better educated young women also tend to enjoy better all-round health and have fewer children. They are more politically active and prioritize the provision of healthcare and education for the next generation. So it must be one of the greatest progressive stories of the twentieth century that during that period the average number of years spent in education increased from six to twelve for men and from five to thirteen for women in the developed world, where countries have made schooling compulsory, usually between a starting age of somewhere between five and seven years old, until the age of between fourteen and sixteen. Thus in the space of just one hundred years, the world's most advanced economies made secondary education the norm for both women and men of all classes.

Understandably therefore, the international community as a whole chose to give significant priority to achieving the prerequisite of universal primary education as the second of its Millennium Development Goals in 2000. While this target was not met, the UN report at the end of that cycle in 2015 should be a source of at least some encouragement. In 2000 in the developing world, 83 per cent of primary-school-age children were enrolled in school. By 2015 this proportion was up to 91 per cent. Of course, when you translate this apparently high percentage into the reality of nearly one in ten primary-school-age children missing out on the most vital of life chances, there is certainly no room for complacency. However, if a working threshold of at least 97 per cent is used to signify universal school enrolment, the target has now been met, or at least almost met, in Eastern Asia and Northern Africa.

Progress, if not yet complete success, was even more dramatic in troubled sub-Saharan Africa, with enrolment figures up from just 52 per cent in 1990 to 60 per cent in 2000 and an even more heartening 80 per cent in 2015. This was notwithstanding a massive increase in the number of small children (86 per cent since 1990), terrible poverty, the scourge of armed conflicts and other emergencies. The real number of enrolled primary school children more than doubled, from 62 million in 1990 to 149 million.

There remained in 2015 the wholly unacceptable figure of 57 million primary-aged children not in school worldwide, though this was down from a staggering 100 million children left out at the turn of the millennium. Poverty and conflict remain obvious and significant obstacles to universal primary education. Further, of the children who are initially out of school, significant percentages (between 43 and 57 per cent, subject to region) will end up never attending.

There is better news when it comes to global literacy, with the percentage of fifteen- to 24-year-olds able to read and write rising from 83 per cent in 1990, to 91 per cent in 2015. Further, broadly speaking, the greater the increase in youth literacy – region by region – the smaller the gap between levels of male and female ability to read and write. Given the enormous joy, solace, entertainment and opportunity that my mother's legacy of literacy has brought to me at every stage of my life, I cannot help but take enormous heart and hope from numbers like these. Unsurprisingly, they are most directly attributable to the increase in primary- and secondary-school attendance.

In terms of gender parity, there were many more girls in school in 2015 than in 2000, and the UN reported that about two-thirds of countries in developing regions had achieved the target of eliminating gender disparity in primary, secondary and tertiary education altogether. In Southern Asia in 1990, there were only seventy-four girls in primary school for every one hundred boys. However, by 2015, this ratio had altered to 103 girls for every one hundred of their male counterparts. The fact that boys are beginning to lag behind girls overall in secondary education in Latin America and the Caribbean is a new and worrying trend. They are also behind in tertiary education in that region, as well as in North Africa, Central, Eastern and South Asia. This seems also to be the case in many countries in the developed world. I would suggest that any such trend should be of no comfort and of real concern to any democrat, let alone feminist, anywhere. Any significant disparity in opportunity or attainment will surely lead to waste, pain and even conflict, among families, communities and societies down the line.

A 2015 OECD report, 'The ABC of Gender Equality in Education: Aptitude, Behaviour, Confidence', demonstrated some dramatic gender gaps between fifteen-year-old boys and girls across the developed world. Boys were reported to be significantly less engaged in their education and more liable to end it early and without qualifications. They were more likely to describe school as a waste of time and to be all-round low achievers. This was attributed to a number of factors. One problem appears to be a masculine stereotype militating against the demonstration of enthusiasm for the school environment. Another seems to be disruptive classroom behaviour, which in turn can lead to the vicious circle of anti-boy teacher bias in the context of school reward and discipline regimes. Excessive playing of video games was also cited, alongside a lack of independent reading for pleasure. However, a moderate level of video gaming that did not interfere with sleep or homework was said to be positively beneficial to the attainment of spacial and computer skills.

Yet, when it comes to numeracy and mathematics, the picture is startlingly different, with girls significantly underperforming compared to boys in most countries. This is especially troubling given the importance of numeracy to the essential life skill that is basic financial literacy, as well as to the further educational and potential professional pursuit of the so-called STEM subjects (science, technology, engineering and maths). Only 14 per cent of women who entered university for the first time in 2012 chose science-related courses. This was in contrast with 39 per cent of the new male students. Further, research suggests that young men are highly likely to make up the literacy gap after leaving school (presumably by taking greater pleasure in their own choice of reading and interest in any written work as a result of further study or employment). Women are less able to address the deficit in numeracy and mathematics by themselves, in young adulthood and the world of higher education or work.

Nonetheless, the significant national and regional variations tend to demonstrate that gender gaps in educational performance are not attributable to anything innate in sexual difference. If boys in the best education systems can outperform girls in reading elsewhere in the world, it must be possible to learn from those systems and societies. If male literacy catches up or even exceeds that of women in the sixteen- to 29-year-old age bracket, young men must be doing something for themselves that school did not achieve earlier on. In particular, on the principle that reading anything is better than not reading at all, it must be possible at an earlier stage to lead boys to reading material better aligned to their own personal interests and abilities; whether cultural, scientific or sport-related.

If girls in Hong Kong, China and Singapore are capable of achieving parity with their male counterparts in maths, and even of doing better than all boys in most other countries of the world, it must be possible to improve girls' mathematical performance everywhere. Further research interestingly shows girls doing better or worse in maths tests depending on what they are told about their purpose. They are said to do better when told that regional comparisons are being made, and worse when they think that their results will be compared to those of male students.

According to the OECD analysis, girls' problems with mathematics are most likely to be highly attributable to a lack of self-confidence and even anxiety relating to the subject. This is particularly observed in the context of problem-solving, applying knowledge and 'thinking like a scientist'. In this type of test, girls across the OECD as a whole are outperformed by boys by a score equivalent to five whole months of schooling. This is in turn attributed to a fear of failure that quickly becomes anxiety around trial and error or experiment. This is a cultural norm that we have surely all seen reflected in the preferences and behaviours of too many of our female friends, relatives and colleagues of different generations, and in so many aspects of life. It is thought to be particularly damaging to the successful study of mathematics and related subjects, especially once crippling levels of anxiety set in and render impossible the kind of thought processes required. Then of course comes the consequential detriment to any earlier or potential aspirations to so many personally and financially rewarding twenty-first-century careers. Nonetheless, the flip-side of this challenge must be of enormous potential gains to a young woman's all-round courage and confidence, once any fear of failure, experimentation and problem-solving is conquered. Further, the research suggests that there are now well-proven teaching techniques for improving confidence around mathematical problem-solving, and of doing so in low-stakes situations where students are less worried about mistakes. Instead, they might be presented with the opportunity to learn from them.

Global and regional statistics, while important, are also inevitably dangerous. The risk is of ironing out significant residual and entrenched problems of very real discrimination against and even harm to girls and women in education. This is true in many individual countries and communities of the world. There is also the danger of becoming blind to the greatest differentiator (even within countries and communities) – the levels of wealth and poverty. Further, the relationship between culture, conflict and the subjugation of girls' and women's access to education is inescapable. The war-torn countries of Syria and Yemen are obvious examples of this. In 2015, the World Economic Forum estimated a literacy rate of 55 per cent for women and 85 per cent for men in Yemen. It reported that only 31 per cent of secondary-school-aged girls were in education, compared with 51 per cent of their male counterparts.

On International Women's Day 2017, Aaron Benavot, the director of UNESCO's Education for All Global Monitoring Report, listed the worst ten countries for female education: Afghanistan, South Sudan, Niger, Burkina Faso, Guinea, Mali, Chad, Pakistan, Benin and Ethiopia. Benavot reported that in these ten jurisdictions, the poorest 20 per cent of women in their early twenties had spent less than a year in school. Six out of ten of that group (12 per cent of young women) had never been to school at all. When he focused on the poorest girls aged between nine and twelve who had never been to school, the list altered slightly. Benin and Ethiopia did slightly better (ranked eleventh and fifteenth worst respectively) and Liberia and Nigeria appeared in the worst ten instead. League tables of this kind make for gruesome reading, not least, as Benavot points out, given the very significant populations of both Nigeria and Pakistan.

The vulnerability of Nigerian girls came under the international spotlight after the infamous kidnap of 276 female students from the Government Secondary School in Chibok by the terrorist group Boko Haram in 2014. It is thought that the girls were taken as trading pawns to be exchanged for Boko Haram prisoners and for use as sex slaves. However, that atrocity has also become a symbol of the denigration of women's rights to education and more generally. There can be little doubt that the targeting of teenage schoolgirls by a group that wishes to establish a caliphate which disapproves of modern education was a crime of highly intentional symbolism. We know that many of the girls have since been raped and forced to marry Boko Haram fighters. Some have contracted HIV and others are said to have been murdered in captivity. In January 2017, as many as 195 of the original 276 students were thought to be still captive, and other girls from the region had been taken in the intervening years. The

Nigerian government has been widely criticized for its inability to protect women and girls in its jurisdiction, and for a lack of urgency in the prioritization of this most basic task of any functioning state. And this despite being ranked twenty-third in the world for GDP by the International Monetary Fund in 2017.

Pakistan is a nuclear power, but still has overall literacy rates of only around 46 per cent for women and 70 per cent for men. This seems a particularly grotesque testament to the judgements around priorities made by some of the powerful who govern our world. There does appear to have been some improvement in the education of younger girls in Pakistan since the shooting of the then fourteen-year-old Malala Yousafzai by the Taliban in 2012, and the global attention which followed. However, according to the charity Plan International in 2015, 60 per cent of Pakistani girls surveyed reported rarely or never feeling confident enough to speak in the presence of boys or men.

Despite having a female president, Liberia, ravaged by conflict and Ebola, has the highest proportion of primary-school-aged children out of school. The UK charity StreetChild began working with street children in Sierra Leone in 2008 and subsequently expanded its ground-breaking integrated social, protection, anti-poverty and educational work to Liberia, Nepal and Nigeria. In Liberia in particular, the organization has provided weekly 'street-corner education' for thousands of children in the capital Monrovia. It is further prioritizing girls' education in the country, where 67 per cent of the girls who drop out do so because of pregnancies, many of which come as a result of sexual abuse, including in school. Liberia has also been targeted for US aid and expert support by the 'Let Girls Learn' programme established under the former Obama administration.

Despite its very low starting point, the world's newest state of South Sudan has some clear plans and priorities when it comes to the education of girls. In 2015, Girls' Education South Sudan (GESS), an initiative of the country's Ministry of General Education and Instruction, reported an overall national literacy rate of 27 per cent and a female rate of only 16 per cent. Girls were more likely to die in childbirth than to complete primary education. This government programme, part-funded by the UK's Department for International Development, has been making direct grants to schoolgirls to enable them to continue with their studies, and to pay for uniforms, books and materials. Capital grants have been made to fund schools themselves so that they do not need to charge prohibitive fees to the poor. Radio programmes have been broadcast with the aim of promoting the value of girls' education to their parents. A short film produced by GESS features young girls in crisp new uniforms, proudly speaking of their ambitions to work towards being engineers in their country in the future. A simple programme perhaps, but a powerful and inspiring one, involving international partnership and an understanding of the vital importance of well-placed funding and parental buy-in in the empowerment of girls. Mobile technology is proving invaluable in monitoring both enrolment and attendance, so that the efficacy of the programme will be measurable over time. In the midst of worsening conflict, GESS is one of the few development programmes that continues to work in South Sudan.

In the worst thirty ranked countries on the list for female education, the poorest girls were getting no more than 3.6 years of education. There remain over 100 million young women in the world who cannot read and write and women and girls are still more likely than men and boys to be excluded from education. The World Bank estimates that 16 million girls aged between six and eleven years old will never start school. The estimate for boys is 8 million.

School is not only a vital place and time for gaining the life skills of literacy, numeracy and other formal academic learning. For most of us, it is an important primary introduction to society, independent of our parents and family. It must always be a place of safety, and sadly sometimes even of refuge. A child's unhappiness may sometimes be shared only with friends or teachers. Scars or bruises inflicted at home are often first detected in a school changing room. For girls in some communities in particular, lengthy absence from school may be symptomatic of forced marriage or other forms of sexual exploitation.

The way that we are treated and learn to treat others in this first or practice community can have a profound effect on how we see ourselves and other people, well into our adult lives. Inevitably, the cultures of these learning environments vary hugely even within communities and nations, let alone worldwide.

I have said how fortunate I feel I was in my own early years. One or two ingrained memories from those days have helped to shape my beliefs about how children and young people should be treated. The first relates to food. As a primary-school child, I can remember the Monday morning roll call that related not just to school attendance but to how our school lunches were going to be provided. The options were as follows. You could have a cooked school lunch for which some brought coins from home in a named, recycled sweet tin. The poorest children only were entitled to a free school lunch. Alternatively, you could bring a packed lunch from home and, for those children with stay-at-home mothers living close enough to the school, there was the choice of going home for the midday meal. I remember the sheer inadequacy of so many lunch boxes. No doubt this is mostly hindsight informed by what I have learned about nutrition later in life. When school catering became privatized, I remember the cheapest and least nutritious options that we as slightly older children were allowed to 'choose' for ourselves. Even more poignantly, I remember children being required publicly to respond to the classroom roll call with the words 'free school meal'.

No doubt such crass insensitivity would not be practised today. Who would dream of requiring small children to self-identify in this manner as being poorer than their classmates? However, given the huge importance of food to physical function and development, and to friendship and community, providing all schoolchildren with healthy, balanced meals must be as fundamental to their education as books and other learning materials. This does not always happen, even in parts of the developed world. Countries like the United Kingdom and United States now have large numbers of children suffering from obesity alongside those displaying signs of hunger and malnutrition. Teenage girls (and an increasing number of boys) also struggle with issues around food and body image. The ideally safe space of school can be a place in which to observe and tackle some of these issues by a combination of discussion, learning and counselling.

The relationship between rules and freedom is obviously another prime foundation of both education and life, but the manner in which discipline is designed and applied can vary widely and with potentially enormous consequences. One of the inevitable challenges of the school environment is that the care of minors does not lend itself to the kind of equal and democratic society that most of us aspire to in adult life.

Yet surely we want school and subsequent education to be a preparation for that very way of living? How to square this circle? How do you bring up children in the inevitable, sensible and logical care and control of the school environment, while nonetheless preparing them to be a great deal more than the good little obedient soldiers, workers and wives of the past? How can you prepare young people for a life of self-discipline, industry and responsibility for others, but also one of self-confidence, challenge and resilience? It is almost an impossible conundrum in the abstract, but we have all seen it achieved to a lesser or greater extent in practice, by the example that school authorities and teachers set with the values they choose to promote and the methods of so doing.

When I was small, the penultimate school sanction short of exclusion or expulsion was some kind of formal beating. This was administered by a senior teacher of one's own sex, via a cane (usually reserved for boys), a ruler or a slipper. I was never beaten at school, but the background threat was always there. I remember it being spoken about in whispered tones by my little friends (at that time, all under twelve years old). We feared both the violence and ritualized humiliation. It was sometimes threatened and often worried about, if much more rarely used, for a host of minor infractions and misdemeanours far short of violence perpetrated by ourselves. It conveyed a form of obedience based on fear, rather than one based on shared values or their understanding. Its eventual obsolescence in 2003 in the United Kingdom (which was late to catch up with most of the rest of Europe) seems to me almost as great a progressive development as universal secondary education itself.

Today such methods of discipline have mercifully been outlawed in most of the developed world, though they continue to be employed in some parts of the United States, Australia and Singapore. This is also the case in much of Africa, Asia and the Middle East. While some entrenched orthodoxy still attempts to justify corporal punishment on the grounds of religion, character development and efficacy, most expert medical and educational opinion pushes in the polar opposite direction. Educationalists and clinicians alike point to it being significantly counterproductive to both learning and behaviour, as well as creating health and psychological risks. I believe that violence breeds violence. Corporal punishment is ripe for abuse by any overheated adult at home, school or any state institution. Conversely, it seems perverse and sadistic when administered by the so-called 'cool hand'. However, moving away from such an overall model of discipline requires far more than simply outlawing the cane or the birch. Even more challenging and therefore exciting is the possibility of converting a traditionally overly harsh, originally male and hierarchically conceived idea of learning into one aimed at fostering all forms of equality, confidence and mutual respect.

I have had the privilege of visiting a great many schools, colleges and universities as a guest speaker over the past fifteen years. Some of these have been incredibly privileged institutions and others a great deal less so. They have been primary, secondary and tertiary, single-sexed and co-educational. The cultures of both discipline and discussion vary significantly and are inevitably hugely influenced by founding values and traditions, as well as the leadership of the head teacher, governors and leadership team. One very important factor in children and girls' empowerment would seem to be how early and consistently they are directly involved in creating both the broader educational experience and the school community itself. I have been to schools of all kinds where an invited speaker is almost sheltered from the pupils, as if out of fear that they might ask a difficult question, appear impolite or otherwise offend. By contrast, I have been greeted, hosted and chaired by groups of even relatively young children in an environment where visionary teachers are attempting to prepare their charges for happy and confident lives and not just the important next stage of exams. There are particularly strong senses of this more confident atmosphere in some of the oldest pioneering girls' schools, which were built to break the mould. Famous founders and strong feminist narratives and values no doubt help to set this tone. However, I have also seen much younger and even relatively deprived urban schools attempting to create brand-new empowering traditions of their own.

An old secondary school friend of mine has spent many years working as a teaching assistant. When I look back at the kind and caring thirteen-year-old I once knew, it doesn't surprise me in the slightest that she should turn to this under-remunerated but crucially important vocation in adult life. Susan Palmer has worked with both primary and secondary school children, including those with special learning needs. One of the professional experiences that she is most positive about and inspired by was an experiment in 'vertical tutoring'. Children aged between eleven and sixteen were grouped together for certain hours of the week instead of spending only formal time in their cohorts. She describes the results as nothing short of amazing. In her own words:

Bullying was reduced and relationships were built. They helped each other with homework and coursework, using their knowledge to assist the younger years and letting the older children realize they were now responsible.

No doubt there are many different versions of this type of approach. Some forms of peer education and supervision have been employed by necessity and because of scarcity of resources in parts of the developing world. Whatever the precise expert framework, it seems to me that there is nothing like being given a little bit of responsibility to practise with and learn from, and being treated with some of the respect that you are expected to show to others, including teachers and peers.

We have long observed the benefits of sport in school, but perhaps concentrated on its function in engaging the energies and developing the discipline of boys. Sometimes the focus may even have been especially on occupying those who were less academically able or inspired. On other occasions, some elite sports have seemed like a golden lottery ticket for the most naturally able. However, as a matter of social and health policy worldwide, we have come to a fuller understanding of the importance of developing healthier lifestyles in general, and of the physical, mental and emotional benefits to girls and women of engaging in sport at school and afterwards. There is now a great deal of research to suggest that even beyond the more obvious long-term health benefits of getting into the regular habit of physical activity, girls who engage in sport are more confident and less likely to suffer from depression, low self-esteem or poor body image. In particular, the experience of being part of a team is thought to be of great social and workplace benefit. Further, these girls are less likely to have an unintended pregnancy and more likely to perform well in school academically and complete secondary education.

It is therefore worrying that in their early teens around twice as many girls drop out of participation in physical exercise as their male peers. This is attributed to factors such as convention and peer pressure, lack of access and role models. In some cases and certain parts of the world, there are even real issues of safety and transport. Surveys also suggest a potential vicious circle of self-critical concerns about inadequate skill, fitness or body size, putting girls and young women off the kind of sporting activity that might actually address all three. This is reminiscent of the fear of failure that we witness with girls and mathematics. However, it can easily be addressed by making more diverse provision for girls of differing skills and aptitudes, so as to enable them to find an activity that works for them. While everyone cannot hope to be a multiple Olympic champion rower like Dame Katherine Grainger or a tennis legend like Serena Williams, these women provide great all-round role models of confident, articulate and resilient womanhood, as well as determination and sporting prowess. So it is important that world-class sporting bodies and media outlets (if necessary nudged by governments) devote equal attention and resources to women's sport.

School cannot do everything, but it can do a great deal to confront the inequalities and stereotypes that persist outside its walls. On International Women's Day, I was asked by another friend to speak at her daughter's co-educational secondary school. A cross-spectrum political panel debated a wide range of issues around gender injustice. I told the story of a recent notorious incident in the House of Commons. A long-standing male Member of Parliament had made animal noises when a younger female colleague had risen to speak. I offered the anecdote with some trepidation, and with the full expectation of at least some laughter from the teenage boys that made up half of the audience. I am glad to say that I could not have been more wrong. I sensed not a single smirk or giggle in the large auditorium. In fact, many of the boys in particular appeared to shake their heads in disgust. I finished with the suggestion that this kind of behaviour would never be tolerated in their school community by the students themselves, let alone the teachers. My albeit extremely limited experience of the general atmosphere made me feel confident about that assertion. Something had clearly gone extremely well in that school, in contrast with some other, even more privileged and advanced places of learning. I cannot help but compare this positive memory with the 'No means yes! Yes means anal!' chants that in 2011 forced the prestigious Yale University to impose a five-year suspension on a male 'fraternity' that had produced five American presidents.

School values, structures, teachers and extra-curricular discussion can clearly play a huge part in shaping our young people's futures, but the curriculum is nonetheless crucial at every stage of our learning. There is still considerable controversy about the wisdom of providing children and young people with age-appropriate sex and relationship education in the United Kingdom and in large parts of the world. Sarah Champion is the Member of Parliament for Rotherham. She campaigned across parties and communities – with ultimate success – for the compulsory inclusion of relationship education in the primary school curriculum in England. She spoke to ITV News in March 2017, putting an argument that is simple, but surely irrefutable in the internet age:

> If we don't have the confidence to give our children proper education about healthy relationships; about boundaries, they are going to go online and find it. What they will find when they type in 'sex' is porn. Do we really want our children to be educated by porn?

In the last century, progressive education systems had enough to contend with, in trying to provide some balance and counter the inadequacies and inequalities that different groups of girls and boys would experience at home. Now in the internet age, they must attempt to counter a whole world of visible inequality. Indeed they must even attempt to provide an antidote to a great deal of poison with which girls and boys, young men and women, are bombarded via twenty-first-century technology and media. It seems to me that there is little choice but to engage in an even more interactive and honest conversation and debate, including around difficult subjects, than ever before. If there is to be space and priority for this exercise, the broad curriculum and materials which support it are key.

Yet researchers and international monitors continue to record the highly gendered nature of too many schools, colleges and classrooms. This can manifest in the unwittingly settled expectations of some teachers, but also in something as basic as the subliminal messages around gender roles and stereotypes found in the images, exercises, problems and examples of so many textbooks for use in different subjects, worldwide. In 2016, UNESCO reported that gender-sensitive textbooks could help enable the discussion of gender stereotypes and inappropriate behaviours. Discriminatory materials could have the very opposite and negatively reinforcing effect, thus limiting the aspirations of girls in school and life. This is hardly surprising given the significant reliance on these materials, estimated as being used in as much as 70 to 95 per cent of classroom time. Women and girls were found to be consistently under-represented, whether measured by lines of text, named characters in titles, citation or indexes.

Studies of Chinese early years' and primary school

textbooks from around 2008 had shown disproportionate male representation. Male characters took up 61 per cent of books for six-year-olds, and despite the full richness of women's role in Chinese history, they featured as only a fifth of the characters in history texts for primary school children. According to UNESCO, social studies textbooks of that time represented all scientists and soldiers as male and all teachers as female. Indian school textbooks were said to feature male-only characters in more than 50 per cent of the illustrations in primary school English, Hindi, maths, science and social studies. By contrast only 6 per cent of the illustrations appeared to feature girls or women only. In maths books in particular, male figures were used to represent commercial and occupational settings, with not a single woman found depicting an executive, engineer or shopkeeper. The same report cited maths textbooks in the Cameroon, Côte d'Ivoire, Togo and Tunisia as featuring no more than 30 per cent female illustrations in the late 2000s, with women and men portrayed in the most traditional stereotyped roles in both the home and workplace contexts. Pakistani textbooks were said to have demonstrated little improvement in the representation of women between 2004 and 2015, and Iranian textbooks in 2012 used male figures as 80 per cent of the characters. A 2009 review of Australian school books showed 57 per cent male characters. Worse still, there were double the number of men depicted in law and order roles and four times as many male characters shown in politics and government.

UNESCO suggested that global institutional and NGO efforts at inspiring change had been frustrated by a low take-up and sense of priority at the level of national governments, public and civil society. However, some positive developments were mentioned. Jordanian school textbooks were now said to portray women as prime ministers and pilots, while some books in both India and Malawi had been developed to challenge students towards discussion by the juxtaposition of stereotypical images next to thought-provoking text. Sweden was especially singled out for special commendation of its 'egalitarian approach to gender in its textbooks'.

Of course education systems around the world will and should have their own offerings of special subjects relating to civics or citizenship, sex and relationship education and so on. These can all play a vital part in preparing girls and boys for happier and healthier personal, social, work and democratic lives. However, a truly progressive curriculum, in my view, would be one in which issues of inequality and diversity are confronted and challenged across the whole spectrum of academic and vocational subjects. This was not commonplace in my own youth, with some rare exceptions via the study of some very specific aspects of the English and French literature syllabus at school, and of law at university. My mother may have introduced me to the life and work of Marie Curie as a pre-schooler, but that was probably my first and last early introduction to a prestigious woman scientist of any discipline. This was despite studying chemistry, physics and biology for public examinations at the age of sixteen and history up to the age of eighteen. In the history teaching of my teenage years, Woman was essentially anonymous. We studied the rise and fall of 'the great dictators' and the birth of the United Nations, with barely a woman's presence in the narrative or commentary – not even, as I recall, Eleanor Roosevelt.

This was obviously many years ago and there would appear to be a great deal more sensitivity to the role of women in the curriculum in 2017. Even so, as late as the end of 2015, campaigners in England were fighting to keep 'feminism' as a strand in the A-level politics course for public examination at around age eighteen. Were it not for a successful high-profile campaign led by national figures such as Trades Union Congress General Secretary Frances O'Grady, Mary Wollstonecraft would have been the only female philosopher on the syllabus. A similar campaign prevailed in relation to female composers on the A-level music course, but other eminent voices in education have made the point across the curriculum, including STEM subjects.

In fairness, one would perhaps expect the teaching of sciences to be more theoretical and practical, but this surely places an even greater responsibility on the teaching and syllabus setting of the arts and humanities – even to encourage girls towards the further pursuit of STEM endeavour. This would involve giving women their fair due for great STEM achievements previously solely attributed to men.

The 2017 American movie *Hidden Figures* is based on a book of the same title by Margot Lee Shetterly from Virginia. It tells the poignant and inspiring story of the African-American female mathematicians ('human computers') who overcame segregation and racism in the US of the 1950s and 60s to become instrumental problem-solvers in the Cold War space race. It is a beautifully told true story of some of the most discriminated-against women of the twentieth century, and shows how the combination of their brilliance, solidarity and hard work, the US legal system and the civil rights movement delivered them their place at the cutting edge of STEM advancement. Their place in history inevitably took longer to be acknowledged, and as a woman born just over a month before that legendary first manned moon landing in 1969, I am rather embarrassed to have discovered their contribution only the best part of five decades later. I can but hope that it will soon be shared with girls on history and politics courses everywhere. This could surely inspire more women to defy all expectations and obstacles, and venture into the world of maths and science.

Rather less inspiring was the sight of an Oxford University examination paper in politics from 2017. It contained twelve questions relating to Marx and Marxism and consequent critique and commentary. Further, one of the questions had two alternative options to address. So there were actually thirteen propositions to play with. Karl Marx himself obviously featured heavily, but the questions also referenced Engels, and called for a consideration of Hegel, Bernstein and Gramsci, the Bolsheviks and Utopian Socialists. Half the human race and any possible interest, perspective or argument that women might bring to these schools of thinking were dealt with in just one question mentioning a woman:

> Rosa Luxemburg's life was undoubtedly dramatic, but her theoretical legacy was slight. Discuss.

Discuss indeed.

Even where women are not the principal protagonists of the story, they might at the least be voices in its telling and subsequent analysis, discussion and debate. Women writers, historians and philosophers should surely feature broadly equally on reading lists for the study of literature and the humanities. If not, why not, other than out of discrimination? The danger is always of the choice of the narrative, nature of the commentary, style of the argument and any eventual conclusions being determined by only one half of humanity, and in truth a much smaller percentage even of that. If we cannot empower our young women and men to challenge the status quo in the classroom, where else will they ever do it, at least via the best, most peaceable and democratic means?

7. Insecurity

Human history has been an extremely violent epic tale, whether the theatre of war was on the domestic, street, community, national or world stage. It would be a school child error, though, to think of women only as victims in all of this, or to erase their role in the prosecution of wars, however righteous or misguided, and in the perpetration of crimes of passion, perversion and profit throughout the ages. Women are certainly more than capable of violence, not least in the cause of defending their loved ones or their own interests. Both legend and history tell of great women warriors from all corners of the globe. Boudicca, Trieu Thi Trinh and Jeanne d'Arc led armies against their Roman, Chinese and English oppressors in the first, third and fifteenth centuries respectively, and women have commanded both royal and pirate fleets. There were female samurai (*onna-bugeisha*) and Apache women fighters like the legendary Lozen, described by her brother Chief Victorio as 'my right hand . . . strong as a man, braver than most, and cunning in strategy. Lozen is a shield to her people.' Women fought in the French and Russian revolutions, the American War of Independence and Civil War and the Irish uprising of 1916. There is a long tradition of women defending the nation in the Nordic countries and in what is now Turkey. In earlier times women often took up arms disguised as men, and were identified only in hospital or after being killed. Sometimes the female sex is seen as its own disguise, so that women are selected as spies, couriers or bombers by resistance or terrorist movements in the belief that they will be less vulnerable to suspicion.

By the Second World War all the main engaged nations used women in uniform, even if they began predominantly in nursing and support roles. By the end of that war, hundreds of thousands were in active combat, whether in anti-aircraft units in Britain and Germany or even in the frontline in the Soviet Union. The anti-aircraft option was seen as a good compromise for combat deployment, as it exposed women to the risk of death but not to the danger of capture by the enemy. Concern about women in the armed forces (what about the poor men?) being captured, tortured and raped seems to be a continuing issue in even modern debates about which kind of active duty might still be inappropriate for them. This fear of capture for military women is notwithstanding the harsh but well evidenced reality of the sexual harassment and abuse they suffer from their own comrades. Then there is the systematic rape of civilian women as a weapon of war, and even the culpability and apparent impunity of UN peace-keepers when it comes to the rape of women and children in conflict and post-conflict zones. In arguments against mixed frontline units or even against having women in the frontline of combat at all, much is said about how men might feel overly protective towards female comrades. Other residual arguments against women in the military refer to our physical weakness, space and privacy constraints, and the 'sexual tension' supposedly created when men and women are put under strain in close quarters.

Some commentators point to the reluctance of men fighting for the so-called Islamic State to give themselves up for interrogation by female enemies. This is countered by those who suggest that women and children civilians caught in conflict are more likely to feel safe and thus to cooperate with women in uniform. Some Western women have become brides of Isis fighters in the Middle East, while others have become volunteers in Kurdish female combat brigades like the YPJ (Women's Protection Units), fighting against Isis with the SDF (Syrian Democratic Forces). In May 2017, Anthony Loyd of the *Times* newspaper wrote about tens of thousands of women fleeing the terror and oppression in Raqqa, once the foremost Isis stronghold, and throwing their black veils and *abayas* into the sand. Ironically, many had experienced particular cruelty at the hands of Isis's female al-Khansa brigade of the Hisbah (morality police). In yet another complex twist of twenty-first-century femininity, many of those fleeing just a few miles to the northwest of Raqqa were likely to be greeted by the fatigue-wearing female fighters of the YPJ. The irony was not lost on the escaping women, one of whom, Um Lamis, told Loyd:

> One minute I lived in Raqqa, a city ruled by men where women had not even the power to show our faces. The next I am greeted by armed Kurdish women, faces bare and their hair uncovered, guns in hands, fighting the daesh. They welcomed me as a sister! I bow to their courage!

Loyd goes on powerfully to describe how this kind of dramatic experience has had an effect on the new governance of villages liberated from Isis control by the SDF. Many now have local assemblies chaired by women. In the words of a thirty-year-old Sunni Arab woman, Amina al-Hassan:

> At first some of the men in my village had a problem when I was elected co-chairwoman to my local assembly. They said it wasn't my place as a woman. So I said to them, to

their faces: 'You didn't dare say a word when the daesh were in charge. Now they have gone you want to deprive women again of their rights?' The men hung their heads.

Loyd's acutely observed account from one of the most dramatic armed and cultural clashes of contemporary times would seem to offer some real optimism as to both the effect on previously oppressed women of a dramatic and visible example of female empowerment, and the potential of men and women who have once lived under tyranny together to fashion a more equal vision of life after liberation.

Women today are found serving in a great many military and para-military functions in most countries of the world. They have been decorated for their courage and skill in many recent wars, but have also been implicated in abuses of power.

There are currently well over 11 million people detained in penal institutions around the globe, whether awaiting trial or after criminal convictions. Less than 7 per cent (700,000) of them are women and 200,000 of those are in the USA. There is no doubt that women have fewer criminal convictions worldwide and even less for violent and sexual crimes. It is widely reported that fraud-related offences account for much female imprisonment. However, the female prison population has grown by 50 per cent since 2000 as compared with only an 18 per cent increase in male inmates. Further, that proportionate increase seems to be evident on every continent. The USA regularly tops the world league of incarceration numbers for men and women. According to the World Prison Population List published by the Institute for Criminal Policy Research at Birkbeck, University of London, in 2016 the country had 698 inmates per 100,000 members of the population, a ratio beaten only by the Seychelles with 799 per 100,000.

This stands against a world ratio of 144 prisoners per 100,000. A large number of the women in prison are mothers, thus creating problems that are no doubt passed down the generations as many lose all contact with their children while in the system. Researchers and prison reformers in the US attribute the recent dramatic increase in the number of incarcerated women to drug use (including acquisitive and drug-related crime conducted in relationships with criminal men). Further, one third of all women in prison there have a serious mental illness. They are predominantly women of colour, on low incomes, and being held pending trial or following conviction for low-level offending.

I would argue that too many women and men are imprisoned, and that the rate of growth in the figures for both sexes worldwide is ultimately unsustainable. Overcrowded and underfunded prisons in particular are often far from 'secure'. Instead they are dangerous places for those employed and detained there. I believe that the trend towards running prisons for profit in some English-speaking countries (Australia, Great Britain, New Zealand, USA and South Africa) creates further risks to security due to cost-cutting and incentivizes increased incarceration. Inevitably, women are even more vulnerable than men in prison, and a greater number of them complain of assaults, including sexual assaults by those entrusted with their imprisonment. If so few of these women have been convicted of serious sexual or violent offences and so many have mental health or addiction problems, one cannot help but wonder whether they would be better dealt with, and the whole of society better protected, even at less expense, if they were both punished and rehabilitated by other means.

In the light of the number of women criminalized for relatively minor or at least non-violent crimes, it seems ironic to say the least, that not all serious violence by and against the female of the species is even universally understood or prosecuted as crime. A perfect example is the 'cutting' or genital mutilation of girls all over the world, either in countries where the practice has been a long-established tradition, or in those to which people have migrated, taking this particular form of child cruelty with them. As of the autumn of 2016, UNICEF estimated that at least 200 million girls and women, living in as many as thirty countries, had undergone female genital mutilation or cutting. In most of these nations, this had been carried out before many of the girls had reached the age of five years old.

The World Health Organization defines female genital mutilation or cutting as follows:

> Type 1 involves the partial or total removal of the clitoris and/or the prepuce (the skin surrounding the head of the clitoris).

> Type 2 is the partial or total removal of the clitoris and labia minora, with or without excision of the labia majora.

> Type 3 is described as the narrowing of the vaginal orifice by cutting and bringing together the labia minora and/or the labia majora to create a type of seal, with or without the excision of the clitoris. In most instances, the cut edges of the labia are stitched together in a practice referred to as 'infibulation'.

> Type 4 refers to all other harmful procedures to the female genitalia for non-medical purposes, for example: pricking, piercing, incising, scraping and cauterization (a medical term for burning).

So far so clinical. Yet move away for just one moment from the impersonal and scientific language. Imagine instead the reality of five-year-old girls being taken individually or en masse, physically pinned down by female relatives (including the mothers who they think of as their natural protectors), while their genitals are attacked with knives, razor blades or scissors. How must that feel for a small child who has yet to have a period or have any inkling of why she is experiencing this violent sexual torture? It is of course designed to keep her chaste before and during marriage, by denying her sexual pleasure on maturity. She endures the brutality and excruciating pain of the childhood experience, without knowing the pain and significant subsequent health risks with which she will be left in later life, on marriage and during sex, childbirth and ever after.

Female genital mutilation or cutting (I resist diluting the brutal truth with the acronym of FGM/C) is particularly prevalent in a broad belt of countries from the Atlantic coast to the Horn of Africa. It is entrenched in Egypt, Iraq and Yemen, but is also practised in various forms in Colombia, India, Malaysia, Oman, Saudi Arabia and the UAE. It also occurs among migrant communities in Europe, Australia and North America.

It goes without saying that this form of conventional and often ritualized torture is contrary to pretty much every international human rights convention that I could list (e.g. the Convention Against Torture and Other Cruel, Inhuman or Degrading Treatment or Punishment, the Convention on the Elimination of All Forms of Discrimination against Women and the Convention on the Rights of the Child). Yet, while it has been in decline over the last thirty years, in no small part thanks to women activists at the international, national, regional and community level, there is stubborn defiance of the progressive trend in many places. UNICEF refers to attitudinal surveys demonstrating majority levels of female support for the continuation of the practice in Gambia, Guinea, Egypt, Mali, Sierra Leone and Somalia, though most of the available data from Africa and the Middle East shows a majority of female opinion in favour of an end to this abuse. But progress is patchy. In *The War on Women*, Sue Lloyd-Roberts writes poignantly of the women she interviews about mutilation and cutting in both the first and developing worlds. She includes a woman facing the refusal of asylum protection in Britain, where she sought to avoid returning to her native Gambia to cut little girls as her mother did before her.

Some things seem clear. However hard it is to talk about this subject, we must acknowledge that it is still too prevalent among Muslims, Christians and people of other faiths in various parts of the world. I don't believe that it should be shrouded in mystery, euphemism or fear of so-called cultural insensitivity. It is grave child abuse and sexual torture plain and simple. If we lack the will and courage to treat it as such in the twenty-first century – whatever the financial and occasional political cost – human rights values mean nothing very much at all. In the meantime, let's not pretend that women do not do violence, even to their own daughters, even if this violence is of the most conformist kind, and out of fear.

For many young girls the risks and the nightmares do not end with cutting and genital mutilation in pre-adolescence. It is thought that more than 700 million women alive today were married as children (i.e. before the age of eighteen). Of them, more than one in three (or 250 million) were married before they were fifteen years old. Inevitably, these child brides are less able to negotiate safe sex effectively and are therefore more vulnerable to STIs including HIV. Others are forced into marriage a little later, or sold – or as good as sold – into sexual or other forms of slavery. The phenomenon is global and most prevalent wherever life is too expensive and/or human life too cheap, and crucially, where institutions upholding and enforcing the Rule of Law are too weak to be an effective protection. In 2016, the World Economic Forum estimated that 45.8 million people worldwide were living in some form of modern slavery, with as many as 58 per cent (or 26.5 million) concentrated in five countries – India, China, Pakistan, Bangladesh and Uzbekistan. If estimates of 55 per cent of slaves being female are correct, that amounts to 25.2 million women and girls. That is more than the total populations of either Australia or North Korea. When it comes to those who have been trafficked across borders, the estimated proportion of women and girls goes up to as much as 70 per cent. Two out of every three child-trafficking victims are believed to be girls.

Not all human bondage is so transparent, dramatic or apparently unusual, though once again it begins early in life. It is estimated that as many as 246 million children experience violence at school every year, with one in four girls saying they never feel comfortable using the toilet facilities at school. This rather depressing statistic comes from a 2015 report by UNESCO'S Education for All and the UN Girls' Education Initiative (UNGEI). Further, while boys can be extremely violent towards each other, girls are at the greater risk of sexual violence, harassment and exploitation. Any physical or emotional abuse in what should be the safe space of the school environment can be extremely damaging to a young person's life chances.

In 2014, in 'Hidden in Plain Sight – a Statistical Analysis of Violence Against Children', UNICEF estimated that a quarter of all girls aged fifteen to nineteen (almost 70 million) had experienced some form of violence since the age of fifteen. The same report suggested that 120 million girls had been subjected to forced intercourse or other sexual acts. There was a considerable geographical variation in this risk, with 10 per cent or more of girls having been forced into sex in most of sub-Saharan Africa. Most of those who had experienced sexual violence had done so for the first time after the age of fifteen, but at least one in five girls in many countries reported at least one incident of sexual violence between the ages of ten and fourteen.

Also in 2014, and according to the EU Agency for Fundamental Rights, one in ten women in the European Union reported experiencing cyber harassment, including of a sexual nature, since the age of fifteen. The risk is thought to be greatest among young women between eighteen and twenty-nine years of age.

Perhaps most depressingly of all, the UNICEF analysis shows that half of all girls aged fifteen to nineteen worldwide (around 126 million) believed that a husband is sometimes justified in hitting or beating his wife. How is a statistic like that possible in the second decade of the twenty-first century, when consensus has grown on the evils of violence against women and there is at least some developing agreement on the ambition of greater gender equality? Why do so many teenage girls still find marital violence acceptable? Perhaps at least some part of the answer lies in the continuing acceptability of corporal punishment by parents against children in so many cultures and even legal systems around the world. If my father or mother as my ultimate authority figures can sometimes be justified in hitting me 'for my own good' when I have done something wrong, perhaps it isn't such an enormous leap of my moral thinking or imagination to accept that the perceived obligations between husband and wife might also sometimes be enforced by violence. No doubt this can be compounded in cultures where there are a large number of young and child brides. If I could be beaten by my father for my misdemeanours yesterday, and I have now been passed from his home to that of my husband, perhaps my husband has acquired the right to physically punish me today? There is also the simple normalization that surely comes with the sheer scale of violence against women in the home. If a young girl has seen her father beat her mother – maybe repeatedly – and her mother has appeared to accept this treatment, perhaps the beating must somehow have been justified in her mind. Further, the converse must be true for little boys too. If violence begets violence, a boy regularly beaten in childhood, or who has watched his mother beaten, may be a little less resistant to giving in to frustrations and violent instincts in the home he later makes for himself and his family.

The UN estimates that 35 per cent of women worldwide have experienced either physical and/or sexual violence by an intimate partner or someone other than a partner at some time in their lives. We do not know how much of the partner violence was sensed or witnessed by any of the women's children, but given the overcrowding of so many people's living arrangements, the numbers must be significant. So is the risk of the violence being somehow accepted and internalized, not only by the women victims themselves, but by the next generation of their families as well. Unsurprisingly therefore, the childhood experience of domestic violence is regularly cited alongside old-fashioned gender norms and male substance and alcohol abuse as key contributing factors in intimate partner violence.

The normalization of domestic violence can hardly be

prevented if and when society, and even the law, sends out mixed messages about it. The concept of rape within marriage was practically an oxymoron in most cultures for millennia. This no doubt stems from notions of women as the property of their husbands (compounded by traditions such as the payment of a bride price) and presumptions of consent to all sexual relations from the moment of entering into the sacrament of marriage. While feminist thinkers such as John Stuart Mill were challenging this thinking and practice as early as the mid-nineteenth century, serious international progress in expressly criminalizing or removing marital defences and exemptions to rape was not made until the latter part of the twentieth.

As late as 1984, a Criminal Law Revision Committee examining sexual offences in England and Wales reported as follows:

> The majority of us . . . believe that rape cannot be considered in the abstract as merely 'sexual intercourse without consent'. The circumstances of rape may be peculiarly grave. This feature is not present in the case of a husband and wife cohabiting with each other when an act of sexual intercourse occurs without the wife's consent.

How does that sentiment strike you, coming as it did from a committee of legal experts five years into the eleven-year premiership of the United Kingdom's first woman prime minister? If rape is not 'merely sexual intercourse without consent', then what is it? Shockingly this thinking is not as rare as it ought to be, even now, more than thirty years later. In 2015, Donald Trump's Special Counsel Michael Cohen responded to media reports that Ivana Trump had accused her former husband of rape, but not, in her words, in the 'criminal sense', during divorce proceedings settled in 1992. Trump has always denied the factual allegations, but his lawyer made the extraordinary further legal assertion:

> And, of course, understand that by the very definition, you can't rape your spouse.

This statement was despite marital rape having been outlawed by all US states by 1993 (twelve years earlier), and by New York State in 1984 (the year of the embarrassing English Criminal Law Revision Committee comments), five years before the incident alleged by the former Mrs Trump.

All of this seems to demonstrate the deeply entrenched notion of a woman as her husband's property, at least when it comes to matters of the bedroom. For a very long time, marital rape was only taken remotely seriously as a potentially criminal matter when accompanied by brutal violence and injury to the woman. This thinking has seeped into notions of 'date rape' being somehow less grave than 'stranger rape', and demonstrates how even changes to the law cannot by themselves always alter deeply rooted societal attitudes.

Of course drugging, abduction, violence and torture should be aggravating factors in the sentencing of rapists, in or outside of marriage or other intimate relationships. Surely these relationships involve a huge mutual trust between those within them? This trust is gravely abused and violated when women (and it is mostly women) are forced to have sex against their will, with or without the threat of violence, within what should be the security of their homes, sometimes even when asleep.

Mercifully the UK story took a positive turn with a lead shown by the Scottish High Court of Justiciary in abolishing the marital immunity in 1989. This was in turn relied upon by the brave, humane and irrepressible judge Simon Brown (who went on to serve with distinction as a Law Lord and Supreme Court Justice, and now sits in the House of Lords as cross-bench peer Lord Brown of Eaton-Under-Heywood), in the marital rape case of R v C, in England and Wales in 1991. The Appellate Committee followed suit later in 1991, in the now legendary case of R v R, dispensing with the 'common law fiction' of implied consent within marriage. The High Court of Australia acted similarly later that same year, as did a raft of other national courts and legislatures in the years that followed.

Speaking in the House of Lords in March 2017, in a debate about the United Kingdom's delay in ratifying the Istanbul Convention on Preventing and Combating Violence against Women and Domestic Violence, Lord Brown said:

> I have few boasts to my name by way of legal achievement, few jewels in my judicial crown, but I can and do boast of being the first judge in this jurisdiction ... to rule that a husband is not permitted in law to have intercourse with his wife quite simply whensoever he chooses – in short, that there is such an offence as marital rape. That decision was said at the time to fly in the face of centuries of established legal principle but in fact, happily, it was upheld by both the Court of Appeal and indeed the Appeal Committee in your Lordships' House.

If you were to meet Simon Brown, with his plummy voice and booming laughter, you might find him a surprising champion of the woman's cause. Yet a champion he undoubtedly is. When judges are under attack by political and media communities, men and women, in the UK or anywhere in the world, I remember that it was an independent, if predominantly male and privileged judiciary, and not a woman-led populist Conservative government with ample legislative opportunity to have done so, that first protected women in England and Wales from rape within marriage.

Progress, however, is neither smooth nor universal. Even accounting for difficulties comparing differing legal systems and practice, there may still be as many as forty countries where marital rape is not fully criminalized, and even more where the law is not properly enforced against husbands or other intimate partners. As the hugely populous China and India are among the nations where rape within marriage is not a criminal offence, the sheer numbers of unprotected women remain a very real concern. Perhaps even more astonishingly, such is the continuing prize of bridal virginity, that there remain a number of countries where a rapist is exempt from prosecution if he makes 'reparation' by marrying his victim. These include Lebanon, Algeria, Tunisia, Iraq, Cameroon and Bahrain, though such laws were prevalent in much of Latin America until the early years of this century. Such an exemption was ended in Morocco in 2014, but only after the high-profile suicide of a sixteen-year-old girl who had been forced by her family to marry her rapist.

By contrast, the Soviet Union was one of the early nations to outlaw marital rape in 1960, alongside Denmark in the same year, following Poland in 1932, Czechoslovakia in 1950 and preceding Sweden and Norway in 1965 and 1971 respectively. How sad and ironic therefore, that contemporary Russia should point in such a contradictory direction on domestic violence. In January 2017, legislators passed a statutory amendment rendering 'moderate' domestic violence resulting in bruising or bleeding rather than broken bones, an administrative rather than a criminal offence. It replaced the previous sanction of up to two years in prison with fifteen days' incarceration or a fine, as long as the offence was perpetrated no more than once a year. The arguments in defence of the change (including from women politicians) related to anomalies of sentencing, with domestic violence arguably being treated more harshly than other forms of violence, and the 'sanctity of the Russian family' (an argument reminiscent of that in favour of the Indian marital rape immunity). There are always real and practical arguments in favour of the availability of restraining and other civil law orders that might seem more attractive options – in family settings – than the criminalization of a loved one. However, civil options should be alternatives rather than complete substitutes for the punishment of violence. Further, critics say that the new Russian law has turned criminal penalties into administrative ones, without simultaneously creating stronger means of restraint and redress for women. It is hard not to see the fine combined with the 'once a year' stipulation as almost an annual licence for domestic violence. And there is the obvious danger that even so-called 'moderate' violence in the emotionally intense and sometimes claustrophobic environment of the home can very quickly escalate out of all control.

'You make me do it!' How many times and in how many languages has a woman heard these words or a close approximation of them? How often has the ominous warning of self-justification rather than real regret gone unheard by anyone but the victim and tragically unheeded by her? In 2012, UN data suggested that of all the women who were the victims of homicide in the world, half were killed by the hand of an intimate partner or family member. For men this figure was only 6 per cent.

One particular manifestation of this is the so-called 'honour killings', a hideous corruption of language if ever there was one. It is hard to get a handle on the scale of this crime, as it is inevitably secretive and inconsistently categorized around the world. It is a particular form of murder and social control that usually involves a group of family members conspiring to punish another (usually but not exclusively female) for expressing sexual freedom (for example, choosing her own partner or refusing an arranged marriage) or other forms of resistance. Where an actual killing is not contemplated or carried out, there might still be brutal violence in the form of beating, abduction, mutilation or acid attack.

Acid violence (even beyond the family 'honour' context) has become an extremely worrying contemporary trend, both on the Indian subcontinent and in Britain, but its full spread is likely to be more international. The desire to disfigure or deface a woman who has spurned either parental power or that of a partner, former partner or stranger is the obvious if perverse flip-side of the woman as prized ornate and reproductive possession. 'If you don't want me, I will make you incapable of being wanted by anyone else.' Acid Survivors Trust International works with volunteers and survivors around the world to combat acid violence (including by scrutinizing and seeking to regulate the supply chain of corrosive substances), and to help rebuild (by surgery and rehabilitation) the lives blighted by this extraordinary cruelty, usually inflicted on the face and upper body, predominantly against women and children.

Psychological abuse is more difficult to measure as its definition can vary across the world, but is believed to be all too common. Rather shockingly, a 2014 survey among the twenty-eight European Union member states revealed 43 per cent of women saying they had experienced some form of psychological violence by an intimate partner at some stage in life. This included abuse such as insults, belittling, repeated humiliation, intimidation (including the destruction of valued possessions), threats of harm and threats to take away or harm children. Such abuse is often accompanied by attempts to control the victim by isolating them from family and friends, monitoring their movements and restricting their access to money and work.

So why do women stay, often for lengthy periods or for ever, in such horrible personal circumstances? It is far too easy from outside the tinted windows of domestic abuse to sneer at the women inside the prison as weak. Sometimes they are disbelieved or harshly judged, even by other women (including self-defining feminists), in the light of their apparent strength, success or confidence in other aspects of life. The international music star Rihanna was perhaps a case in point. Neither money nor children were an issue when she returned at the age of twenty, if only briefly, to her violently abusive boyfriend. Her November 2009 interview with ABC's legendary broadcaster Diane Sawyer is as illuminating as it is moving. Encouraged by clear but sensitive questioning, the young singer talks with dignity and lucidity about the shock and embarrassment of being the victim of intimate physical assault. She describes guilty feelings that it might have somehow been her fault, initial concerns about the well-being of her ex-boyfriend, and then recounts witnessing assaults by her father on her mother in her own childhood. 'Love is so blind . . .' she told Sawyer before indicating that it was, at least in part, a sense of responsibility towards her young women and girl fans that ultimately encouraged her to leave the relationship:

The broken arm; the black eye, is gonna heal. That's not the problem. Its the scar inside.

More positively, the immediate aftermath of the airing of the interview was a 59 per cent increase in calls to the US Domestic Violence Hotline. Given the millions of viewings which the interview has subsequently achieved online, one can only imagine and hope that it has been a source of strength and inspiration for many more women everywhere in the years that have followed.

There are perfectly rational and understandable reasons for a reluctance to end a particular episode in one's family life, however violent or abusive. Concern for children is an obvious factor. Some women fantasize about leaving a bullying partner once children are grown and independent. They may worry in the interim about family stability, economic insecurity and social stigma for themselves and their children if they escape too soon. A lack of independent economic means is likely to be an obvious issue for a woman with or without children. Alternatively, a woman may be worried that she will be deprived of custody of or access to her children. Men often threaten this (as do women), whether or not they mean to follow through. She may fear other, including violent, means of retaliation or isolation from family and friends. Finally, there is the highly possible reason of continuing love, even for a violent and abusive partner and the hope or belief that things will change.

Despite all the countervailing pressures, many women do eventually leave. According to the World Health Organization, this is often after many attempts at escape and many years of violence. Factors in the decision to go permanently seem understandably to include an escalation in the severity of the violence, the realization that the abusive partner is not going to change and the recognition that the violence is affecting the children. So children are, at least ostensibly, one of the primary motivations for women in abusive relationships, initially to stay and eventually to go. Much has been written about the relationship between poverty and intimate partner abuse. There does seem to be evidence of a greater prevalence of it in circumstances where men lack other resources and mechanisms to live up to entrenched stereotypes of power and control. On the other hand there is also evidence that wealthier men may be more likely to engage in abuse of a psychological and controlling nature, and that women who acquire independent economic power may create a challenge to their partners that can itself generate tensions within the home environment. Further, there have always been high-profile examples of rich, powerful and highly educated men physically abusing their partners. Across cultures and classes, isolation of women and couples would seem to be one key factor in both continuing domestic abuse and a woman's inability to escape it. This can in part be alleviated by family and other informal support systems. But at this point in the twenty-first century, it surely demands adequate financial, social, legal and counselling support and refuge for those living in fear and seeking to escape it.

If home is not safe and secure, neither is the outside world. A 2012 UN 'Safe Cities' study reported that in New Delhi 92 per cent of women were subjected to some form of sexual violence in public spaces during their lifetime, and 88 per cent experienced behaviour such as sexual comments, wolf-whistling, leering or obscene gestures. The on-street experience of women is appreciably different from that of men the world over. Men are no doubt the greatest perpetrators and victims of violence in public places, but the female experience of sexualized abuse and violence is greater. There is clearly a complex relationship between law and culture with neither sphere holding the magic bullet to tackling social evils. We do need law and the resources to enforce it, but also the education and campaigning that will give this and future generations of men and women the confidence to change our own behaviours, stand up to abuse in private and public and offer support to those in need. We must make this a constant and clear political priority.

If women are vulnerable to violence in general, some are even more so. There is strong evidence to suggest the increased vulnerability of women caused by factors such as sexual orientation, disability and ethnicity, as well as in the high-risk contexts of humanitarian crises, conflict and post-conflict situations.

The United Nations High Commissioner for Refugees (UNHCR) currently reports the highest levels of displaced people on record: 65.3 million people are thought to have been forced away from their homes at a rate of up to 34,000 people worldwide each day. The UNHCR recognizes 21.3 million of these as refugees (according to the tightly drawn and even more tightly interpreted 1951 Refugee Convention). Half of them are believed to be under the age of eighteen.

Half the people caught up in this humanitarian crisis of unprecedented proportions are women and girls, with their increased vulnerability. Displaced women in camps and other refuges suffer disproportionately from disempowerment, sexual and gender-based violence, a lack of legal redress, education, economic self-reliance and individual documentation, without which it is almost impossible to rebuild their lives in a secure new home country in the medium- or longer-term future. Health and reproductive care are particular problems for women refugees, not least in some of the sprawling and degrading camps that have become a characteristic feature of our twenty-first-century world. The most flimsy and insecure shelter makes rape and what the UNHCR terms 'survival sex' an all too common and increasingly accepted way of life for many displaced women and girls, even after they have escaped to affluent first world countries, to differing levels of acceptance or hostility.

Too many have to flee for reasons related to their sex and gender in the first place, and then face additional risks thereafter. These include some quite small children who arrive in supposedly safe destination countries unaccompanied and vulnerable to sceptical and resistant authorities and malign criminals and traffickers. What must it feel like to be a mother so scared for the imminent future that you put your child in a boat, or lorry, or otherwise into the hands of strangers, knowing you will most likely never meet again? What does it feel like to be a child in a refugee camp or reception centre anywhere in the world, with no idea as to whether your mother is alive or dead? This is the reality for millions of people and we have yet to come up with sufficient international consensus in either foreign, trade, military or humanitarian policy (let alone their interconnection), to scratch the surface of the problem.

Rape has been a systematic weapon for terrorizing populations in the DRC for over twenty years since Rwanda invaded the country in 1996. As veteran feminist campaigner Gloria Steinem says in the opening to a May 2016 episode of the Viceland documentary 'WOMAN':

> Rape in times of war is a form of terrorism designed to instil fear, create trauma and destroy communities. The victims are attacked, mutilated and then shunned.

While hostilities have long formally ended, the most brutal and debilitating gang rape has become normalized by all sides in the post-conflict situation in the DRC. Whole communities of widowed and shunned women and children of gang rape struggle to survive with the most basic of farming and mining methods while continuing to live in permanent fear of further attack. The normalization of rape has spread beyond former conflict zones and the militia and into civilian society. Despite the country being rich in mineral wealth, or perhaps actually because of this fact, lawlessness and impunity continue. Rape is used as a means of creating fear and flight from precious lands which could otherwise be mined and harvested for the good of the whole population in a society built on more effective governance. There must be a greater responsibility on international corporate consumers of coltan (whose by-products go into so many of the world's electronic products), to exert a positive rather than a corrupting influence on those ruling the country.

Steinem's colleagues report that of the 1.8 million Congolese rapes of the last two decades only a handful have resulted in prosecutions and that there are hundreds of new hospital cases every month. Yet the film is far from completely bleak. It features the strong voices of survivors turned counsellors and activists, such as the late Masika Katsuva, and distinguished medical professionals like Nobel Laureate Dr Denis Mukwege. They are well-armed with insights into a proud but scarred population, well aware of the possibility of a future built upon human rights and the Rule of Law. What is needed is that vital combination of legal structure and psychological support that has provided at least some semblance of a solution after other traumatic long-term conflicts.

Women need not be the perennial victims of war. They are also capable of being the architects and agents of the peace. I do not want to fall into the trap of stereotyping us always as the natural conciliators and diplomats on account of either biology or conditioning. I have cited many violent examples to the contrary. However, there is real evidence from across history and around the globe of the value of women's involvement in peace-building. Perhaps it helps to mix up the conversation and its voices? Perhaps it can be especially beneficial after sustained conflict to create potential coalitions of interest and experience along lines other than those (nationality, race, tribe, religion or politics) that have been the previous basis for war? In any event, greater equality around the table and in the settlement is surely more likely to lead to a more sustainable peace and security.

Perhaps the germ of the idea is as old as Aristophanes' play *Lysistrata* from 411 BC. The comedy tells the story of a woman who leads the women of Greece in a sex strike against their menfolk in order to force them to negotiate an end to the Peloponnesian War. No gentle, compliant diplomacy here, but full-blown sanctions of the most intimate kind. Eleanor Roosevelt was the wartime First Lady of the United States from the beginnings of Nazi rule in Germany in 1933 to the end of the Second World War in 1945. It is her peace-building role for which she will perhaps be longest remembered. As the US delegate to the UN General Assembly from 1945 to 1952, she was a principal instigator and architect of the Universal Declaration on Human Rights, designed as much for world peace as for individual justice:

Whereas it is essential, if man is not to be compelled to have recourse, as a last resort, to rebellion against tyranny and oppression, that human rights should be protected by the rule of law,

Whereas it is essential to promote the development of friendly relations between nations,

More poetry than practice in today's insecure world perhaps, but still enough for her late husband's successor, President Harry Truman, to describe her as the 'First Lady to the world'. Enough too to give continuing solace, inspiration and legitimacy to women and men all over the world to build a peace based on freedom and equality.

Women have also played a vital peace-building role in Liberia, where they were heavily involved in the peace talks before standing for election as democratic representatives, and Colombia, where they took their courage in their hands to campaign against the civil war and even negotiate with armed guerrillas. Finally, in a dramatic symbol of hope, just across the border from the still troubled DRC, women were first peace-makers and then leaders in post-conflict Rwanda. After that country's conflict and genocide in the 1990s, women decided that orphans were not Tutsi or Hutu but children in need of adoption. Now those women sit in positions of power in a peaceful state in what is currently the most female parliament. This must surely suggest a similar potential contribution by women in advancing greater peace, security and equality all over the world.

8. Faith

If gender inequality is the greatest global injustice, there are increasing points of resistance and progress. It may not even be an exaggeration to describe an accelerating movement for change right now, nearly a fifth of the way into the twenty-first century. This movement is everywhere, including in the sometimes underestimated realms of faith, which have made important contributions to women's lives and advancement – not least via education – throughout the ages. However, one cannot ignore the way in which the great world religions have all too often clung to their less progressive cultural and scriptural roots in the distant past, and stood in the way of women's rights and equality. This they have done, both within their own faith communities and in wider society, all over the world. Worse still, and once more too often, women and girls have been actively denigrated and abused by members of the religious communities and leaderships in whom they had placed so much of their faith and trust.

Margaret Atwood's legendary dystopian novel of 1985, *The Handmaid's Tale*, has made a timely comeback in 2017, thanks to the strong production values and performances of a Hulu TV drama based on the book. It is set in a totalitarian Christian fundamentalist theocracy that was once New England in the United States. Women's rights are quickly wiped out and a population shortage – the result of sterility brought about by pollution and STDs – causes the military dictatorship to turn the few reproductive women into 'handmaids' or sex slaves at the service of the Republic of Gilead. It is a well-told story now angering and inspiring a whole new generation of women, all the more powerful for its universal truths about how the holy texts of any great credo may be so easily appropriated by those who seek to subjugate women.

This is not to say that the rights of women cannot be squared with freedom of faith, conscience and religion. That is not what I believe. Both are essential pillars of human rights thinking and democratic development, and most importantly a great many women, including feminist women, cherish their faith. Yet, the times are changing, and the necessary negotiations must develop with them, if irreconcilable conflict and rupture are to be avoided within the great faiths. Religious freedom must include the right to the faith of one's choice, the right to no faith whatsoever, and even or perhaps especially, the right to hold and express apparently heretical views within a faith discourse at any time. This is especially important when it comes to the rights of women. For the witch or other female heretic of one moment or century may well become the saint or sage of the future faith.

It seems to me at least, that the religious communities most capable of evolving and embracing women's equal dignity will be the ones that continue to survive, thrive and make relevant and positive contributions to the lives of individual women, men and whole societies. It is not for me, though, but for the keepers of the various flames themselves ultimately to decide whether women's equality is something which their consciences and communities can countenance, or better still, wholeheartedly pursue. Laws of our various lands, informed by universal human rights values, can and should impose principles of equality on faith organizations' commercial and charitable interactions with the wider world. This is particularly important when the care and education of children are involved. But when it comes to religious doctrine and the core practice of any faith in question, as a matter of both ethics and efficacy, progressive change must come from within.

It is neither 'unenlightened' nor old-fashioned to respect the role of faith and its communities in the world. For to do so is to respect human beings in all of their beautiful and occasionally contradictory complexity. Whether notionally or actively religious or not, we are all creatures of faith and reason, emotion and logic. The most devout practitioner of any religion will, no doubt, make a great many important decisions on the basis of some kind of calculation. At the very least, whenever there is food to be shared and time and resources to be allotted and spent, rational decisions are constantly being made without any resort to prayer whatsoever. Similarly, the most brilliant secular rationalists will sometimes make hugely important choices about who they like, love and even choose to share their lives with, without the slightest recourse to hard evidence or careful calculation. This is just how most of us seem to be.

Faith and religion play an important part in a great many lives, and people take different things from them. A Gallup survey from 2012 showed 59 per cent of the world self-identifying as religious, but religious traditions and institutions probably carry a much greater influence than is reflected in even this majority percentage of active participation in global faith. They leave their marks on the structure of family, wider society and even legal and political norms long after we can readily identify the original source. Feminists, however privileged, progressive, cosmopolitan and intellectual, ignore this relationship with the reality of so many women's lives at our peril. The three broad components of the offering appear to be some combination of a spiritual dimension for the self, an ethical and often social or even legal code for living and lastly some kind of active, passive or mere sense of participation in fellowship and community. In different places and at different times, women can do better or worse under each of these three elements in all the religions and their great many sects and denominations. For many women, faith is a vital part of their life experience and even their personal identity.

Faith has given billions of women a route into reflection, literacy and wider learning. It has provided many with purpose, fellowship and celebratory ritual at various stages of their lives. It provides solace for many through the trials of life and, most crucially perhaps, at times of bereavement and death. This soothing balm is something that many women have described failing to find in the secular world, or at least not in sufficient abundance, regularity or consistency. However, the power of faith leadership and communities can also be used very dramatically to hamper and even positively harm women's lives. In the twenty-first century, old men, whether they come with or without beards or books, simply have no right to enforce unequal and bad marriage and divorce arrangements, or impede sex education, contraception and reproductive safety. They may not promote unchallenged the degradation and torture that is wife- and child-beating, *chhaupadi* and FGM. Nor should women continue to be the forever fearful, loyal or even enthusiastic handmaidens of the denigration of their sisters and daughters.

Christianity remains the faith with the most global adherents (around 2.2 billion souls). It is estimated as likely to be so for some years yet. It is not for me to argue the theological basis for either the subordination or equality of women within the Church, but there are many others who are well qualified to do so, and it is important to recognize that these debates still rage. There is much argument about how the role of women in the early founding days of the faith was either underwritten by the male authors, curators and interpreters of the New Testament, or most likely actively suppressed. However, recent years have seen a reappraisal of the contribution of women to the early Church, including the rehabilitation and greater recognition of Mary Magdalene and the inclusion of too long forgotten early Christian women. Scholars inevitably continue to trade biblical references from Old and New Testaments in support of either the equal or lesser (or at least differentiated) role of women in the Church, family and society. Should women really submit to their husbands and be silent in church? These sentiments (or perhaps they were edicts) are famously to be found in some of St Paul's letters. However, St Paul also declared:

> There is neither Jew nor Greek, there is neither slave nor free, there is neither male nor female, for you are all one in Jesus Christ (Galatians 3:28).

When it comes to the first Book of Genesis, a great deal is inevitably made by many of Eve as the second rather than the first human, and of her role in Adam's disobedience and the subsequent Fall of Man. This was plainly not lost on Mary Wollstonecraft's daughter Mary Shelley in her framing of Frankenstein and his unhappy creation, who then wants a companion. Multiple Marys are as much a feature of feminism as of Christianity. The masculinity of the Holy Trinity is also an issue for a great many, but by no means all Christians. Increasing numbers of practitioners seem perfectly happy to think of God as above and beyond sex, gender and even sexuality. There are strong voices within the Anglican communion and other Churches of an egalitarian and even feminist tradition. This is neither new nor particularly surprising. So-called 'first wave feminism', or the movements for women's suffrage and property rights in the US and UK in particular, was well populated by Christian women. I am no great surfer of the sea or the net and don't delight in the 'wave' jargon much. As with first and second cousins of whatever remove, it's too easy to forget the generational and other relationships of this short-hand of the initiated. Furthermore, the image of waves crashing onto the beach, but inevitably falling back and dis-appearing, is a less than optimistic one for what we are striving to achieve with greater equality.

In any event, Christian suffragettes and their tamer suf-fragist cousins were able to draw on the social justice and even arguably feminist elements of Jesus' life and teaching. Women's Temperance movements were a large part of this struggle and indeed even their temperance ideals had a femin-ist motive. For the argument was that it was women and children who bore the social and economic brunt of exces-sive drinking. Further, there was a long and rich history of women and even working-class women preaching and taking up other leadership roles within some of the more evangel-ical nonconformist Churches. Sometimes, though far from always, the anti-hierarchical and democratic instincts of these denominations have had collateral benefits for women's equality. These women included some whose work eventu-ally took them from Britain to the New World, and others who were sent as missionaries to do evangelical, education and health work in Africa and Asia. The Salvation Army was founded in 1865 by Catherine and William Booth. Both preached and put the women and men of their Church on an equal footing from the start. Women were first received into the full ministry of the Methodist Church in 1974 and Kath-leen Richardson was elected the Methodist Conference's first female president in 1992.

Despite the faith-based feminism of so much of the suffrage movement, the real rub between feminism and much of Christianity inevitably came with first, the claims for women's reproductive rights in the 1960s and 70s, and then the ambitions of women seeking to take up greater leadership roles within the Church itself. Some women, as with adherents of any belief system, became disillusioned and left or lapsed as a result. Many others remained, though, and continue with their attempts to develop their spiritual convictions alongside or even indistinguishable from their egalitarian ones. They still seek to advance the contribution and understanding of women in all branches of Christianity.

I met a woman many years ago, before women were allowed into the ministry of the Church of England. She was a kind person, a social progressive. I found her articulate and able to challenge and be challenged in discussion and respect rival points of view. I immediately understood why the ministry, with its reflective, scholarly, pastoral and advocacy functions, should appeal to her and other women. I will never forget her describing with some passion how hard it was to feel 'hated within a community that you love'. I had never before been so directly confronted with the plight of the heretic, whether a woman, or an LGBT person or just someone with a different point of view, within any long-standing belief system. I am glad to give witness that the woman in question has long since been ordained as a vicar, and that there are now ten women bishops in the Church of England. In the United States, Katharine Jefferts Schori spent nine years from 2006 as the presiding bishop of the Episcopal Church and was therefore the first woman Primate of the Anglican Communion. Some say that developments like these could never happen in the Catholic and Orthodox churches, but there are long-standing arguments and campaigns for full equality, even in these apparently more conservative branches of Christianity. Meanwhile, the following words of Pope Francis from January 2014 continue to excite discussion, speculation and even hope among many women and men of his global flock:

> I too have considered the indispensable contribution of women in society. I have rejoiced in seeing many women sharing some pastoral responsibility with priests in accompanying people, families and groups, as in theological reflection, and I have expressed my hope that greater room can be made for a more capillary and incisive female presence in the Church.

A couple of years later, though, in answer to a journalist in November 2016, Pope Francis appeared to shut the door, at least perhaps for the period of his papacy, on what many feminist Catholics see as the ultimate equal recognition, which would come with the full ordination of women into the priesthood.

Islam is another monotheistic Abrahamic faith. It currently has the second largest number of followers worldwide (estimated at around 1.8 billion), though its youthful demographics and population growth projections suggest that it may well overtake Christianity's numbers within three to five decades. This dramatic growth, alongside events since the 9/11 atrocity in New York in 2001, have of course heightened the scrutiny of a faith whose name some people quite literally translate as meaning 'peace'. The place and treatment of women is under particular scrutiny and is hotly debated and contested from within and outside, with varying levels of good and ill will around the world.

I am writing this passage barely a week after the horrific murder of twenty-two people by a single 22-year-old suicide bomber at a pop concert in Manchester. Seventeen of the victims were women and girls; nine were teenagers, and one of those killed was a little girl aged just eight years old. The predominance of young and female victims in this death toll cannot have been a coincidence for the attack was not directed against a security or military establishment, but a pop concert. What's more, the artist performing on 22 May 2017 was Ariana Grande, a young woman singer, well known for having an especially strong teenage and pre-teenage female following. Diverse communities in Britain have stood together against terrorism many times in the past. We will no doubt do so again, but anti-Muslim sentiment has been expressed online and even in parts of the mainstream media. A critical world gaze has turned towards Islam once more and millions of my fellow Britons (many of them women, so often more readily identifiable, due to observant dress) understandably fear suspicion, isolation and even abusive or violent recrimination.

Contemporary Western perceptions of this religion are too often simplistic and ignorant of the wide diversity of its various groupings and male and female followers worldwide. As with Christianity, there are many self-avowed feminists – men and women – among its ranks. Of course, there are also a great many individuals and groupings with an extremely traditional view of the appropriate place of women in the family, faith and world. Many mosques still exclude women from worship and some, but by no means all, practitioners hold strong views around the segregation of the sexes in prayer and other settings. Again, as with Christianity, there are women, not least those who have been oppressed and abused, who found the faith of their birth to be ultimately irreconcilable with their modern worldview. Faith is like that. There are also an increasing number of women converts, including in Western, largely Christian countries like the United Kingdom. Some of them describe previously hedonistic lifestyles which left them feeling empty or alone. Others report feeling somehow better protected and respected within the faith and even at times by way of modest garb such as the headscarf. It would seem clear that there is no more one definitive Islam than there is one Christianity, or a single version of feminist thought. And it can sometimes be as difficult as it is important to attempt to separate historic cultural customs from core tenets of any particular faith.

The Moroccan sociologist and writer Fatema Mernissi is sometimes described as the founder of Islamic feminism. She is perhaps most famous for her 1991 book *The Veil and the Male Elite: A Feminist Interpretation of Women's Rights in Islam*. In this work she drew on the skills and traditions of both her sociological and Islamic scholarship to argue against misogynistic readings of the Qur'an and hadith. These include not trusting your business affairs to women and excluding them from the sacred space. Such interpretations, often citing hadith from the Prophet Mohammed's companions, would have been worthy of St Paul's less enlightened moments. Mernissi argues that these are at odds with the prophet's original and overriding egalitarian intent. She maintains that the prophet never intended women to be either veiled or excluded from religious or public life, and cites both his inclusion of his own wives in public discussion and support for women's rights to inheritance. Muslim feminists often remind us of the prophet's first and substantially older wife, Khadija, who brought him into her business. Mernissi also cites this famous verse of the Qur'an itself:

Indeed, the Muslim men and Muslim women, the believing men and believing women, the obedient men and obedient women, the truthful men and truthful women, the patient men and patient women, the humble men and humble women, the charitable men and charitable women, the fasting men and fasting women, the men who guard their private parts and the women who do so, and the men who remember Allah often and the women who do so – for them Allah has prepared forgiveness and a great reward. (33:35)

Similarly, my irrepressible friend Sayeeda Warsi approached the state of women in modern British Islam in her book *The Enemy Within* (Allen Lane, 2017). Baroness Warsi is both a practising Sunni Barelwi Muslim and a Conservative politician. She served in the coalition government from 2010 to 2014, and resigned over what she described as its 'morally indefensible' position on the bombardment of Gaza. She and I have much in common, not least that we are both self-identifying feminists, daughters of migrants from the Indian subcontinent, lawyers and active proponents of universal human rights. As the first British Muslim Cabinet minister, who was at various times Conservative Party chair, Senior Minister of State in the Foreign and Commonwealth Office and Minister for Faith and Communities, Warsi, you might well say, has earned the right to speak frankly to her faith community and be given a considered hearing in return.

In her powerful personal and political story, Sayeeda Warsi tells of her first marriage to a cousin under the auspices of a traditional imam:

Many years later, when I married my second husband, Iftikhar, the ceremony had two important differences: it was conducted in English and it felt right.

In a chapter entitled 'The Muslims', Warsi addresses her 'dear co-religionists' with a call to action to shape and embrace a truly twenty-first-century British Islam. She champions the acceptance of a greater diversity of opinion and debate, and in particular of improving the position of women. She urges men not just to respect their mothers, but all women and girls. She writes against the continued informal practice of polygamy, the poorer religious educational provision for girls, non-legally formalized marriage, which leaves so many women unprotected on separation, forced marriage and FGM:

> For me, Islam is the faith that gave women a separate legal and economic identity, not simply as chattels of their fathers and husbands as they were in Britain until the 1800s. Women in Islam right from its inception played a major part in forming the faith, playing an equal role in business, trade, in politics, as jurists, academics, scholars, physicians and even in battle.

Happily, my friend is far from alone in a feminist discourse both within this faith and inspired by it. Susan Carland is an Australian academic, broadcaster and the author of *Fighting Hislam: Women, Faith and Sexism*. She is seeking to create space for Muslim women's own authentic and diverse voices, and thus to move away from what she sees as the polarized and distorted discourse between fundamentalist patriarchs on the one hand, and 'western feminists' outside the faith.

> It is as though male Muslim scholars and non-Muslim western feminists have handed down predetermined scripts

for us to live by. And it is left to those people thought not to exist – Muslim women who fight sexism – to rewrite those scenarios and reclaim our identities.

Carland, a convert from the age of nineteen, chooses to wear a headscarf, and Warsi, born and raised within a Muslim family, does not. However, Warsi says that four of the five daughters of her parents have worn the hijab at some point. She describes similar diversity in the prayer patterns of her various sisters. Few topics seem to spark as much instinctive and at times even irrational heated debate as Muslim women's clothing. Right and far-right European politicians have attacked and even outlawed the burka, niqab and, in some contexts, the hijab as well. This they have done, in my view, in the worst traditions of dog-whistle politics, while pretending a muscular feminism and secularism that they seem less interested in pursuing in relation to a host of gender injustices, especially when non-Muslim women are concerned.

In my last book, *On Liberty*, I described once being castigated by a tabloid newspaper for being a 'so-called feminist' because I did not support calls for the banning of the burka in Britain. On the day that the story of my failed feminism and hypocrisy ran, the journalist in question very kindly called me for a comment. No doubt, any mealy-mouthed liberal waffle or thin-skinned feminist rage on my part might have provoked ridicule and grist to the mill for a 'day 2' story. I thanked the journalist for the phone call and offered something along the following lines: 'My feminist heart does not leap with joy when I see a woman covered from head to toe in a shroud. But nor does it leap at the sight of a young girl with her breasts bared on the pages of your paper.'

Unsurprisingly perhaps, my comment never ran in the newspaper, and a couple of years ago the topless pictures stopped appearing as well. However, I often think of this incident as a reminder to myself of the dangers of imposing my particular preferences for dress codes on other women, or men for that matter. Of course, we should discuss and debate why some of us sometimes, or even always, wear ridiculously high- or pointy-heeled uncomfortable shoes. I shall never forget the irony of walking into the London première of the great feminist film *Suffragette* behind immaculately dressed young women who literally could not walk in their shoes without male assistance. Feminists and all women have always debated shoes and make-up. We discuss when and how and what to cover or not, as a matter of fashion, freedom, the prevention of skin cancer or pursuit of vitamin D. It is surely just a public and even political development of getting dressed for an evening out in the safety and privacy of a friend or sister's bedroom. We try on various outfits to enthusiastic approval, friendly but cautionary advice, or hoots of laughter.

However, no matter how much I may privately disagree with the choices you make about your clothing, I would be reluctant publicly to criticize you for them (as happens to far too many women in public life), let alone to legislate for dress. The exceptions to this aspect of free expression would be where the proper performance of a public or occupational role truly requires the wearing or removal of certain items. This might, for example, mean that the language teacher of small children should not cover her mouth, or that a witness in court might be asked to remove a full face veil for part of her testimony. It no doubt requires polite and discreet body searches at airports or other places of high security. Nevertheless, as with speech, I think it extremely dangerous to ban items of clothing because they challenge our sensitivities or even offend us.

Of course the counter-argument rests upon a woman not really having free will in so many family and other situations. The fear is of a woman or girl effectively being forced to dress in a certain way by those at home, whether men, women or both. This is a very difficult question because so many of us, even supposedly educated, empowered and articulate feminists, have at times felt pressured to do things that were not really of our own choosing. This is bound to be the case with some girls and women and some religious dress codes, and by no means just within Islam. However, I simply cannot assume this to always be the case. To do so seems to me to be profoundly anti-feminist. How dare I doubt the capacity of another (particularly a fellow adult) woman freely to make choices about religious observance and appropriate clothing, just because they are different or even diametrically opposed to my own?

Ironically, though, I think the argument against clothing bans becomes even more powerful when you test it against the hypothetical assumption that a woman has actually been disempowered by her family and community. What if a woman really is subject to the brutal control of father, husband or brothers? If you suspect there are bruises under her burka, why on earth would you ban her from dressing that way in public, so as inevitably to leave her trapped at home? Disempowered women of any faith and none surely need the greatest opportunities to engage with other women beyond the narrow confines of family and immediate community, and especially in educational spaces? This is what ultimately saddens and angers me the most about the rise of burka, niqab and hijab bans in our so very enlightened Europe of recent times. They are obviously counterproductive to the liberation of any woman who is truly under the thumb of male relatives and faith leaders. You may argue that you are criminalizing the symbols of women's oppression, but you are in fact criminalizing the woman and perhaps even ultimately forcing her to choose between your official prison and the informal prison of her own home. Both the fact that such bans have been accompanied by passionate political speeches about national or Western values and identity, and the banning of minarets in mosque design in Switzerland appear to suggest a blatant culture war, rather than any genuinely feminist motive. It would seem that in culture wars, as so often in conventional military campaigns, women can too easily become both justification for ill-judged intervention and consequent collateral damage.

As with other religions, debate continues, with perhaps renewed twenty-first-century vigour, as to the permissibility of women leading others (whether women only or mixed congregations) in prayer. Women imams and other scholars and guides are now regularly leading worship in a number of mosques around the globe. We can detect far more than the rumblings of a movement away from segregation in prayer and full equality between women and men.

Judaism is the oldest, but now by far the smallest, of the three main Abrahamic faiths (with perhaps around 15 million adherents worldwide, subject to definition). It is by no means any less rich, complex and diverse, including in the context of debates over the role of women. Many still point to segregation in worship and complications around religious divorce as a challenge to equality among some Orthodox Jewry. However, every denomination of Judaism would now seem to contain its own feminist strand of thinking and discourse, and women rabbis have been common and leading mixed congregations for many years. As in Christianity, some feminist practitioners of the faith (men and women scholars) reinterpret ancient texts with a more gender neutral perception, though this can at times prove controversial. Reform Judaism, in particular, promotes a very firm stand in favour of gender equality, including reproductive rights and sex education. Further, its official website explicitly cites the Talmud in condemning marital rape. As I discuss elsewhere, this is in startling contrast with the shameful delay of some legal systems built on other faith foundations in tackling the issue, even today.

Hinduism is the third most populous world religion (with about 1.1 billion followers). It is also said to be the oldest, though it is described by some as less a religion than a broader way of life. It is most prevalent in Asia and is followed by the majority of the populations of India, Nepal and Mauritius. It is enormously diverse, not least for having no central authorities, governing bodies, prophets or traditional or gendered ecclesiastical orders comparable with those found in the Abrahamic faiths. It seems both fascinating and perhaps contradictory from a feminist point of view. On the one hand, its multiple representations of the deity in both strong female and male forms seem readily to lend themselves to an intellectual and spiritual gender neutrality and practical equality. There is no need for mental gymnastics to access a female version of God here. The divine feminine is ever-present. On the other, some of the strong patriarchal and even misogynistic practices and huge social and economic inequalities of the countries where Hindus are most numerous seem to sit in significant contrast with some of the tales and texts of apparent gender harmony and equality of the Vedic period of its roots. As always therefore, scholars, commentators, practitioners and activists must work hard in their discourse to separate man-made traditions (especially those harmful to women) from divine inspiration, and cultural customs from the desired tenets of the creed.

The sheer antiquity of Hinduism makes authenticating various versions of ancient texts extremely difficult. Some describe eight versions of marriage, including both a woman's arranged marriage by her father, and a man and woman finding each other without parental (or any other party) involvement. Crucially, practices such as the now obsolete *sati*, where a devoted widow threw herself on her dead husband's funeral pyre, and even dowry payments, are today widely viewed as subsequent cultural developments rather than scriptural or originally practised by the faithful. Nor does gender preference or selection within families, discussed elsewhere, seem to have any foundation in faith, rather than the circumstances of power and inequality over time.

As with the other great world religions, adherents of both sexes take a whole range of positions in various debates around women's equality. There are Hindu women who simply and strongly self-identify as feminists without further description or qualification. There are others who do not. Further, as with their Muslim sisters, there are some women who feel that so-called 'western feminism' does not adequately understand or represent them and who are therefore seeking to carve out a faith-inspired and culturally sensitive feminism of their own. The discourse is taking place in the first post-colonial century, and against a backdrop of various ethnic and religious nationalisms around the world.

Buddhism also originated in Ancient India. Most of its 500 or so million followers are now elsewhere, including many Western converts (men and women). Around half the world's Buddhists are to be found in China, and it is the dominant religion of Bhutan, Myanmar, Cambodia, Tibet, Laos, Mongolia, Sri Lanka and Thailand. Significant populations also exist in Japan and across the Far East. As with other faiths, the teachings and example of the Buddha are seen as sometimes contradictory in their approach to women. There are unsurprising instructions towards wifely obedience, but paired with the requirement for men to respect their wives. The Buddha accepted women into his monastic community, but with certain restrictions on participation. Scholars refer to aspects of misogyny in early Buddhism, but ultimately focus on the genderless nature of the nirvana or enlightenment at its heart. Women are said to have been ordained throughout Buddhist history, and there has been a resurgence of this in recent times. In 2009, the Dalai Lama referred to himself as a feminist and has more than once suggested that more women leaders would lead to a more peaceful world. He has even positively speculated about the possibility of a female Dalai Lama, though perhaps spoiling the feminist fun with comments to both Larry King in 2014 and Clive Myrie (BBC) a year later, that '. . . that female must be attractive'.

The global Sikh community is currently estimated at around 27 million people. Sikhism was originally pioneered as a deliberately egalitarian (not least casteless) faith by a succession of ten Gurus. God (or Nirguna) is described in gender neutral terms and there was always supposed to be full equality between men and women within the community, including in all matters of participation and leadership in prayer. The first Guru, Nanak Dev Ji, is said to have been a particularly strong advocate of the improvement of the woman's lot in the Punjab of the 1400s and the following teaching is often cited by followers of the faith:

In a woman, man is conceived, from a woman, he is born . . . why denounce her, the one from whom even kings are born? From a woman, women are born. None may exist without woman.

It is extraordinary to imagine these words coming from a fifteenth-century male religious leader anywhere in the world, rather than a twenty-first-century feminist polemic. Subsequent Gurus outlawed polygamy, *sati*, female infanticide and restrictions on women's dress and promoted equal education. Further, the name Kaur was bestowed on Sikh women so that they should not have to take a husband's family name on marriage. Many of these teachings have been too often forgotten or ignored in the centuries that followed. Even today, the rates of infanticide, dowry payments and the denial of education to Sikh girls in the Punjab are thought to be high, even against general rates in India. Many young Sikh women of the diaspora still feel treated as anything but the equals, let alone warriors of their original heritage. This conflict between an explicitly egalitarian religious doctrine and misogyny of cultural practice presents a real dilemma for a great many Sikh women. Many remain spiritual warriors nonetheless, and continue to fight for their space, both within the faith and well beyond it. There are few better examples among them than my friend British Sikh film director Gurinder Chadha, with her wonderful cinematic treatments of the woman's experience in works such as *Bhaji on the Beach* (1993), *Bend It Like Beckham* (2002) and *Viceroy's House* (2017).

My invitation to feminist women and men would be to spare a thought and a modicum of understanding for women of faith. Perhaps they should even be offered a little of the space and solidarity that they are struggling to obtain from some fellow members of their religious communities. Why should we do this, even if we think that some of those struggles are ill-conceived or even doomed? Because believing in equality has to include respecting difference. Because we are not seeking to replace harsh, judgemental and overly exclusive orthodoxies with new ones of our own. Because, like it or not, faith is a force in the world. As long as that is the case, the world can only be improved with every success of those striving from within that force to make it better for women.

My suggestion to religious leaders, institutions and communities of faith is simple and far from original. It may not be my place to make it, but it comes in the spirit of critical friendship and dialogue. You are important to a great many women. Equally, you have relied on their devotion and patience for millennia. Such reliance once seemed your right, but then perhaps it became habit, calculation and even gamble. Nonetheless, the patience itself was for those women alone to bestow. Where they are being oppressed and even persecuted in the wider world by those claiming the false justification of faith, you can surely seek to protect them. In the end, if you choose or feel compelled explicitly to reject, or even subtly distance your work and faith from a wider global drive for equality, progressive women and men will see it and make their choices. They may submit or collaborate, or wait a bit longer, at least for a time. They may continue to struggle against the perceived injustices of their faith family, with whatever degree of discretion, dismay or disquiet, from within. They may more publicly agitate and even splinter or split the religious community. Or these good people – often motivated in no small part by the sense of justice that their religious conviction, alongside other influences, has inspired in them – may eventually leave you, as others have done before. If they feel compelled so to do, many of us believe that you and your community will be poorer, smaller, less relevant, resilient, self-critical and therefore sustainable as a result. So why not keep faith with them?

Conclusion

A world in which we are all equal is one where women and men share power, responsibility and opportunity. It is potentially a happier and more peaceful world, where women are less likely to be harmed by an intimate or loved one and men are less likely to die at the hands of another man or by suicide. It is a world where all people have the freedom to be self-defining and where those definitions matter less and less as the most important distinction increasingly becomes that of being human. A less unequal world precludes the concentration of wealth and influence in so few hands that even democratically elected politicians and apparently fearless journalists flinch from speaking truth to what is currently all too unaccountable true twenty-first-century power.

To be blunt, it is for anyone to decide whether to describe themselves as a woman or a feminist. Yet I reserve the right to be a little more critical of a self-proclaimed feminist woman or man who does not stand up for equality, inclusion and human rights (beyond their own narrow self-interest), than of any self-defined woman who can or cannot boast a particular physical characteristic, or life chance or experience. I have enjoyed many book groups and drinks parties, but the struggle for gender justice asks for a social engagement of a completely different order. It is not a 'single issue'. It cannot be separated from politics and economics in the deepest and broadest sense, nor from fundamental rights, both civil and political, social and economic, at home and abroad. It cannot be achieved within our comfort zones, or by talking only to people like ourselves.

A fairer world is a place where sex-selective abortion is neither encouraged nor facilitated by societies and ethical medical professionals. It is a place where advances in reproductive medical science, no matter how welcome, are not commoditized to the point of some parents seeking or being allowed to pre-select or design the sex of their unborn to suit either whim or wallpaper. It is also a place where the wallpaper need not be pink, blue or otherwise stereotyped.

We should fight against the over-gendering of babies' and children's toys, clothes and especially their books and aspirations. We should achieve this by campaigning, consumer action and public education and childcare procurement policy. Remember the power of boycotts in bringing down another apartheid in the last century.

Politics and politicians who trash or belittle women should be called out by all democrats, no matter how powerful the state which they lead or aspire to lead. We don't have to do politics that way, and misogyny is no better than racism. We have to talk about the internet. It is not being sufficiently policed, even within the parameters of existing international and domestic law. Police and law enforcement authorities around the globe should be better resourced so as to leave no ungovernable Wild West territory where death and rape threats and incitement to sexual and violent crime go completely without or without adequate consequence. Further, the corporates who are busy colonizing and monetizing our online world should also be held to account. If they are not prepared to create platforms and environments of sufficient safety, nation states and international bodies working in concert, and individual users and entrepreneurs (of which a great number will be feminist men and women) should consider appropriate legal and consumer interventions or the development and promotion of alternative ethical cyber-spaces.

Old-world media needs to step up as well. A combination of public service provision, investment and intervention, ethical corporate governance and consumer action could be employed to achieve broad gender parity in film and TV. If not now, then when? If not us, then who? I have no doubt that one day people will watch old feature films and television programmes of the early twenty-first century, with their predominance of men of a certain age, race and persuasion, with as much gentle amusement as some of us now listen to the Received Pronunciation and view the dinner suits of an earlier age. If you read this and feel uncomfortable, speak to someone appreciably younger than you who doesn't want your patronage. Check both your privilege and your jacket at the door.

Affirmative action in the form of some kind of temporary measures to speed up equal representation (whether in legislatures, judiciaries, corporate governance or the workforce) is not an evil in itself. Seeing it as evil is predicated upon a notion that the status quo in the world is somehow meritocratic. If you have taken the time and trouble to read all that came before this Conclusion, and are still of that view, I can only apologize for failing you. However, you may as well believe that slavery was once meritocratic too. By definition, anyone reading this book (and I include its author) is a relatively privileged person. We can read, which probably means we were in education – and for some years. We have access to books, either by purchase, personal loan or by educational or public library. So many people in the world still do not. This is not the product of anything that anyone might remotely describe as meritocracy. Accidents of birth and the exploitation of others soon become a shoulder-shrugging complacency about inequality that comes with the soothing pill that makes us lucky ones feel that it was somehow our entitlement, or that at least it wasn't our fault. Yet, with greater global education, empowerment and communication than ever before, how can we continue to pretend? This does not mean the creation of permanent quotas. I do not support that kind of monolith – not least because I believe that we can aspire to make sex and gender difference less important as we progress. I agree with Article 4 of the 1979 United Nations Convention on the Elimination of All Forms of Discrimination Against Women (CEDAW). Temporary measures to kick-start change need not be entrenched. Instead, it is my view, experience and observation that within a short time of a significant transformation in the representation of women, a consequent change in culture and expectation can come about.

Indeed, we can already see the benefits of taking positive action in the legislatures which achieve the greatest gender equality. Rwanda has been the best example to date with constitutional gender quota requirements. However, non-constitutional action by specific political parties has achieved 47.6 per cent female representation in Iceland's single house. Further, the UK House of Commons' best yet catch of women members in 2017 came not as a result of single issue campaigns or parties, but in no small measure because of an integrated feminist social justice policy across the Labour Party programme and a substantial number of all-women shortlists for Labour parliamentary candidate selection across the country. Of the 208 women elected (still only 32 per cent of the total of 650 House of Commons' representatives), 119 – more than half the women – were Labour. That was greater than all the other parties put together. These women constituted 45 per cent of our party's representation. By contrast, the Conservatives delivered only sixty-seven women and 21 per cent of their seats. Figureheads at the pinnacles of politics – especially those who do not advocate, or substantially advocate, policies for greater equality – are no substitute for greater feminist policy and representation all the way across the horizon and all the way deep down the well.

Outside the machinery of democratic governance, discrepancies in female emancipation and representation are even harder to justify. These should therefore be even easier to remedy. Freedom of conscience does, it seems to me, preclude democrats from imposing measures such as women-only shortlists on political parties that simply do not believe, or sufficiently believe, in women's equality. That ethical problem could of course be avoided, if there were enough broad democratic support in any state for constitutional amendments which require a certain number of women representatives in a particular legislative chamber. The parties with strong enough objections could freely choose simply to absent themselves from these competitions by not running sufficient numbers of female candidates.

No such problems arise, in my view, in either the apparatus of the judiciary or of corporate governance. Both seats of power play a vital role in any democratic society built upon the Rule of Law. Thus democratic society is entitled to demand an element of demographic equality and diversity of representation. This is in order both to improve the decision-making and crucially the legitimacy and long-term sustainability of the institutions. I have found no rational evidence or argument, as opposed to fear and prejudice, to suggest that such measures need interfere with either the quality or independence of these vital structures. Once more, any form of affirmative action could be experimental and time-limited, but the current pace of progress is simply lamentable in too many parts of the world.

Gender injustice is structural, social and economic. It is not merely either accidental or formal, civil or political. I have found that there are too many countries the world over where women appear to enjoy all sorts of exquisite rights to equality under constitutional instruments and statutes, in theory. Important though these are, they prove wholly inadequate without a practical approach to wealth and work that revalues women's contribution and potential. Domestic labour needs to be measured and counted. This may be achieved by sharing or supporting it as regards women and men within the home environment and beyond. It may also be addressed by guaranteeing people a minimum income and standard of living, even when they choose to take on a greater domestic (and often caring) burden. We need to see children, the elderly and the disabled as our shared societal responsibility. A decent progressive, healthy and wealthy society must be judged by how it treats the vulnerable and the collective provision that it makes for them. There must be more free and affordable caring provision to suit women's and men's working lives, hours and aspirations, as well as the dignity, potential and quality of life of those in need of constant or regular care. Work in the caring professions should be better valued and remunerated and we should aspire to greater gender balance therein. Should it really be that investment banking is regarded as of such an exponentially greater value than teaching or palliative care? More democratically accountable and decent societies can surely go at least some way towards redressing the profound imbalance.

Concrete and entrenched obstructions to women moving around in safety and working equally in the world should be addressed. Democratic nations must incorporate speaking the truth about women's rights and the violations of these (however inconvenient this may be), with powerful trading partners and diplomatic allies. Overt discrimination against half of humankind in political representation, employment, ownership, inheritance, land and family law is not a 'cultural' peculiarity to be excused or ignored on account of oil, religion or tradition. It is simply unacceptable in any twenty-first-century family of nations and must be a priority for the UN. Investment in physical infrastructure as well as social infrastructure benefits gender justice. Worldwide, women have even greater need of safe streets, public transport, adequate social and affordable housing, policing and access to real justice.

Employment and equality laws need more, not fewer teeth, in the face of all the whining about regulation being an inherently bad thing. Ethical businesses, whether small, national or international, should not and do not aspire to a race to the bottom in taxation, pay, discrimination and other vital employment, environmental and consumer protections. They rather see their place and importance in making a better world, but need a more level playing field. Employment and especially equal pay legislation should not rely upon enforcement by individual employees alone. Companies are legal creations of the state that benefit from it just as individuals do. It is not unreasonable to require greater transparency, audit and enforcement of equal pay laws by appropriate state authorities, as is the case with taxation and other aspects of corporate governance.

We must be far less complacent about all forms of vertical and horizontal segregation and discrimination in labour markets. We should see it as something strange and unhealthy rather than something that we have come to expect and accept. A whole host of encouragements and programmes might be employed in differing economies to address drastic deficits in either male or female representation in any particular workplace or profession. Again, if a public policy or industry case can be made in any one sector at any particular moment, there should be the legal possibility of varying forms of affirmative action to galvanize transformation, inclusion and greater parity. Trade unions are capable of being key to these conversations both at industry, national and international levels, but these immensely important movements must also address their own occasional instances of social and gender conservatism so as to promote more women, especially in relation to sectors and unions where women are increasingly numerous among those represented.

Public health policy and provision, reproductive rights and care are vital to the basic well-being, let alone any aspiration of greater equality for women globally. This must include scientifically accurate, age-appropriate and non-judgemental sex and relationship education from early on in the life and development of boys and girls. Sex education does not lead to premature sexual activity. Indeed, there is plenty of evidence pointing to it delaying first experiences until a young person feels better prepared for the potential health and emotional consequences and responsibilities. I defend the right of social and religious conservatives and others to promote both abstinence until marriage and fidelity within it. However, this freedom of conscience and expression cannot come at the expense of a child's or young person's right to learn the basic biology of their bodies, and how to keep themselves protected from unwanted pregnancy, HIV/AIDS and other STDs. It may now seem a rather dated technology, but the humble condom remains as important to public health in this century as it was in the last.

In mature democracies and even beyond, we ought to be better at talking about menstruation and menopause. The female reproductive cycle has a huge impact on so much of women's working, social, physical and emotional lives that it needs to be liberated from the embarrassing margins of private conversations to a more central place in public policy and discourse for the benefit of women and men. Advertising is already beginning to play a more positive role, but so might education, ethical employment practice, tax and public health policy and so on. Sales taxes on feminine hygiene products are discriminatory and completely unacceptable. Conversely, free provision of such products in places of work and learning should be explored. Contraceptive education and advice are vital for boys, girls, women and men worldwide. Abortion should of course be regulated, not least to ensure the medically qualified and safe treatment of women. On the other hand, whatever the perennial personal ethical dilemmas surrounding the beginning and end of human life, women should not face criminalization for making choices about their own bodies. Equally, overall maternal health and safe deliveries should continue to be a greater public priority. It is not a luxury to be paid for and profited from but a fundamental human right.

Mental health provision should no longer be the 'Cinderella service' of public health policy. It is no exaggeration to suggest that it has the potential to positively shape, heal and even save lives, families and whole societies. A less unequal world could aspire to the availability of free, or at least affordable, qualified counselling for everyone, whether provided at school, workplace or community level. It should not be a remedy of last resort, but as much a part of a healthy life as good nutrition or regular exercise. True enough, some people resort to the gym when seeking to lose weight or rehabilitate after an illness or injury, but once this goal is achieved, many keep going in recognition of the continuing benefits to overall health and well-being. The same may be true of the 'emotional gym'. In every other aspect of public health provision as well, we should return to the 1948 World Health Organization definition of health as 'a state of complete physical, mental and social well-being and not merely the absence of disease or infirmity'.

The concept of 'home' can encompass so many things for people. At the very least it must surely involve both structural and emotional shelter and even nurture. Adequate housing is a human right and not the commodity that too many powerful people on our planet have allowed it to become at disastrous cost to people's lives and national and international economies. As in other aspects of life, women appear to suffer the most from both the physical and economic insecurity that inadequate housing provision creates. Many countries would benefit from greater legal intervention to protect women's rights to housing. The rights of widows to inherit and keep the family home are a particularly urgent priority in many parts. There should be greater regulation of housing markets and standards and more social housing so that this fundamental human right may be realized for everyone.

Greater free and affordable childcare provision is capable of improving the lives of women and children everywhere. It can help children learn to play, work and live with others, both peers and carers. Crucially, it can give women real choices and the power to explore and employ their own potential outside the home and domestic relationships which should never feel like prison. Creative twenty-first-century public policy (whether planning, social or childcare) could explore means of fostering intergenerational connection, support and community in contrast with so much of the atomization and isolation that was such a feature of the late twentieth century at least in parts of the urban developed world.

A woman's place in and outside her family cannot be a free and happy one without practical and emotional equality in her intimate relationships and financial independence outside them. Democratic states and modern economies should actively pursue women's economic security. It should begin with the aspirations of girls at school, continue with greater professional and labour market equality, extend into appropriate provision of childcare and social care and potential minimum incomes. Women and men should also have access to free or affordable legal advice and redress on divorce, bereavement, unemployment, homelessness and the other potentially devastating events in life that can leave people feeling disempowered, trapped and lonely. As families, communities and national and international societies, we can all better care and provide for each other in the natural, constructed and emotional or inner worlds which we all inhabit.

Learning is vital. I would even venture to suggest that a happy and healthy life includes some kind of learning from beginning to end. Getting as many people as possible into full-time education throughout childhood and even more than a little beyond is one of the most positive aspirations for our planet. What goes on inside school is equally important. Literacy and confidence around or even love of reading are the most enormous gift to any boy or girl. Any gaps in attainment should be constantly and consciously watched and addressed. This is equally true in the context of the language of numbers and of mathematics as the gateway to the so-called STEM subjects that could offer so much more mental, professional and economic stimulation and power for women than is currently the case worldwide.

Educational environments should also be safe places, offering good nutrition. Even the most excellent teaching will struggle to impact on a child's mind inside a hungry, malnourished or beaten body. Policies of free and healthy school meals (lunches and even perhaps breakfasts), for young children in particular, are capable of making an enormous difference to the lives and life chances of many of the poorest children and mothers. So-called 'corporal punishment' has no more place in school than domestic violence has in the home. Healthy educational environments and government and other programmes can also encourage the continued participation of teenage girls in exercise and sport with their longer-term life habits, health and broader confidence in mind. Gender justice is an ambition that should be interwoven with every aspect of school culture, curriculum and materials. Feminism isn't a specialist subject to be crowbarred into one little module of a civics or politics course. It is a way of living and thinking from which every aspect of life, and therefore the educational curriculum of boys and girls and undergraduate, postgraduate and vocational students, could benefit.

Acknowledging and confronting violence against women must include challenging women not to participate in the cutting, premature and forced marriage and enslavement of their daughters, sisters, nieces and daughters-in-law. Nor is violence against children a good way of breaking cycles of violence between men and women in the home or in wider society. The tackling of all forms of domestic abuse requires greater priority and resource globally. Women need places and networks of safety. Ultimately, civil and administrative measures can only ever be a supplement to, not a substitute for, the protection of the criminal law. Rape is rape and a terrible crime, in or outside marriage or other intimate relationship. For a twenty-first-century state not to criminalize marital rape is a horrific violation of human rights and should be so treated by friendly nations, trading partners and the entire international community. Rape as a weapon of terror is a war crime and should be treated as such. Women, having too often been among the worst victims of conflict in the home, on the street and in the world, may have a vital and exciting role to play as architects of the peace. Peacemakers and nation-builders should ensure that the woman's voice is always to be found, and found in sufficient number, at every table of post-conflict resolution.

Faith communities from the local to the global must find their own way to a resolution between their scriptures and traditions on the one hand, and the twenty-first-century universal human rights consensus around women's equality on the other. This kind of discussion, development and accommodation can ultimately come only from within religious groups, communities and institutions themselves. The world is watching. It would ultimately seem short-sighted for such communities of belief and sad for so many women within them, if this challenge was not taken up with both courage and love.

The process of writing this book has been an extraordinary privilege and adventure. It has coincided with a time of considerable tumult in the world. It has been a sobering, sad and at times even enraging experience to read and hear of the lot of too many women and girls and boys and men the world over. For them, fear of powerlessness, poverty, sickness, destitution, isolation, illiteracy, insecurity and violence remains a constant condition.

Nevertheless, my journey has also been one towards

greater optimism. For every expression of prejudice, division, hate, greed and entitlement, there is a counter-narrative of curiosity, unity, love, solidarity and equality. For every story of injustice, including the many I have recounted here, there is another one of heroism and hope. Yes, technology can be used to watch, enslave, abuse or incite us, but it can be used to inform and empower us as well. Frightened and angry people can turn on each other, but there is plenty of evidence all around of their capacity to come together in order to achieve more positive change. Of course too much wealth, health and power are enjoyed by too few, but the ballot box and representative democracy, street and online protests, civil society and trade union action and the law are still enormously powerful levers for change. As we have seen in recent times in several places, it is possible for us to come together as women and men, young and old, at home and internationally and use the power, talents and hard-won rights and freedoms that we have to build a fairer settlement. I believe that far greater equality for women and men is realistically within our reach and well worth the stretch.

Further Reading and Viewing

1. Prayer Before Birth

Amartya Sen, 'More than 100 million women are missing', *The New York Review of Books*, 1990

India's Daughter, film directed by Leslee Udwin, 2015

Rita Banerji, 'A deadly politics of wealth: femicide in India', *openDemocracy*, 2 August 2016

Sue Lloyd-Roberts, *The War on Women* (Simon & Schuster, 2016)

Flavia Krause-Jackson, 'In South Sudan, brides cost plenty – in cows', *Bloomberg Businessweek*, 4 August 2011

Jing-Bao Nie, 'Non-medical sex-selective abortion in China', *British Medical Bulletin*, vol. 98, no. 1, pp. 7–20, 2011

Christophe Guilmoto, 'Sex imbalances at birth: current trends, consequences and policy implications', United Nations Population Fund (UNFPA) Asia and Pacific Regional Office, 2012

World Health Organization (WHO), Preventing Gender-biased Sex Selection: An Interagency Statement OHCHR, UNFPA, UNICEF, UN Women and WHO, 2011

Council of Europe, Convention for the Protection of Human Rights and Dignity of the Human Being with Regard to the Application of Biology and Medicine: Convention on Human Rights and Biomedicine, Treaty no. 164, 1999

Frank Newport, 'Americans prefer boys to girls, just as they did in 1941', Gallup, 2011

Cordelia Fine, *Testosterone Rex* (Icon, 2017)

C. N. Lester, *Trans Like Me* (Little, Brown Book Group, 2017)

Simone de Beauvoir, *The Second Sex* (Knopf, 1953)

Mary Wollstonecraft, *A Vindication of the Rights of Women* (J. Johnson, 1792)

Kwame Anthony Appiah, '"But would that still be me?" Notes on gender, "race", ethnicity as sources of "identity"', *The Journal of Philosophy*, vol. 87, no. 10, pp. 493–9, 1990

Judith Butler, *Gender Trouble: Feminism and the Subversion of Identity* (Routledge, 1990)

2. Misrepresentation

Rebecca Solnit, 'From lying to leering', *London Review of Books*, vol. 39, no. 2, pp. 3–7, 2017

CNN, '2016 US presidential election exit polls', 23 November 2016

Suffragette, film directed by Sarah Gavron, 2015

The Everyday Sexism Project – http://everydaysexism.com

Leke Sanusi, 'Using mapping and Twitter to fight rape in Syria', Vice (Women's Media Centre), 4 March 2013

Ultraviolet (digital campaigning group) – https://weareultraviolet.org/about-us

The Representation Project – http://therepresentationproject.org/about

What Women Want, film directed by Nancy Meyers, 2000

Caroline Criado-Perez, *Do It Like a Woman* (Portobello Books Ltd, 2015)

Diane Abbott, 'I fought racism and misogyny to become an MP. The fight is getting harder', *Guardian*, 14 February 2017

Geena Davies Institute on Gender and Media, 'The reel truth: Women aren't seen or heard', 2016

Miss Representation, documentary directed by Jennifer Siebel Newsom, 2011

Nicola Slawson, 'Ethiopian music scheme loses UK aid funding after press criticism', *Guardian*, 7 January 2017

United Nations Children's Fund (UNICEF), A Statistical Snapshot of Violence Against Adolescent Girls, 2014

United Nations Women, Facts and Figures: Leadership and Political Participation – Women in Parliament, 2016

3. Wealth and Production

James Keir Hardie, *From Serfdom to Socialism* (G. Allen, 1907)

Oxfam, 'An economy for the 99 per cent', 2017

United Nations Department for Economic and Social Affairs, The World's Women 2015: Trends and Statistics, 2015

Aeschylus, *Seven Against Thebes*, 467 BC

Henrik Ibsen, *A Doll's House* (1879)

Mary Wollstonecraft, *A Vindication of the Rights of Women* (J. Johnson, 1792)

In Time, film directed by Andrew Niccol, 2011

Alfred Marshall, *Principles of Economics* (Macmillan and Co., 1890)

Charlotte Perkins Gilman, *Women and Economics – A Study of the Economic Relation Between Men and Women as a Factor in Social Evolution* (Small, Maynard & Company, 1898)

Marilyn Waring, *If Women Counted* (Harper & Row, 1988)

Monique Villa, 'Women own less than 20 per cent of world's land. It's time to give them equal property rights', address to the World Economic Forum Annual Meeting, 2017

Cheryl Doss, Caren Grown and Carmen Diana Deere, 'Gender and asset ownership: a guide to collecting individual-level data', World Bank Group, Policy Research Working Paper no. 4704, 2008

The World Bank, Women Business and the Law 2016: Getting to Equal, 2015

United Nations (UN), Report on Fourth World Conference on Women, Beijing, 4–15 September 1995, 1996

United Nations Department of Economic and Social Affairs, Trends in Contraceptive Use Worldwide 2015, 2015

US National Partnership for Women and Families, America's Women and the Wage Gap, factsheet, 2017

International Labour Organization (ILO), Towards a Better Future for Women and Work, Gallup, 2017

Queen of Katwe, film directed by Mira Nair, 2016

International Trade Union Confederation (ITUC), Investing in the Care Economy: A Gender Analysis of Employment Stimulus in Seven OECD Countries, 2016

Women's Budget Group, AFS 2016: Women's Budget Group Response, 2016

Diane Elson, 'Gender equality and Europe's future', European Union conference, 2003

Kate Bellamy, 'Gender budgeting', background paper for the Council of Europe's network of experts on gender budgeting, Women's Budget Group, 2002

Debbie Budlender and Guy Hewitt, *Gender Budgets Make More Cents: Country Studies and Good Practice* (Commonwealth Secretariat, 2002)

Feridoun Sarraf, 'Gender-responsive government budgeting', International Monetary Fund, working paper 03 (83), 2003

Rhonda Sharp, 'Budgeting for equity: Gender budget initiatives within a framework of performance orientated budgeting', UN Women, 2003

House of Commons Library, Estimating the Gender Impact of Tax and Benefits Changes, SN06758, 2016

Sarah Champion, 'The government preaches equality so why do cuts fall on women?', *New Statesman*, 1 March 2017

ILO, Equal Remuneration Convention (no. 100), 1951

United States House of Representatives, The Equal Pay Act, vol. 29 of the United States Code, at section 206(d), 1963

Parliament of United Kingdom, Equal Pay Act, 1970

World Economic Forum, The Global Gender Gap Report 2016, 2016

International Trade Union Confederation (ITUC), Achieving Gender Equality, 2008

Office for National Statistics, Annual Survey of Hours and Earnings: 2016 Provisional Results, 2016

Peter Shadbolt, 'The sign of the bat: with an original mission of raising people from poverty, why has microfinance become so controversial?', *CFA Magazine*, May–June 2012

'Silicon Valley's sexism problem', *The Economist*, 15 April 2017

Morningstar Manager Analysts, 'Fund management fails to become more female friendly', 2016

The Henry J. Kaiser Family Foundation, 'Distribution of physicians by gender', State Health Facts, 2016

The American Bar Association Commission, A Current Glance at Women in the Law, 2017

Catalyst, Women in Law in Canada and the US, 2017

The Council of Europe, 'European judicial systems: Efficiency and quality of justice', *CEPEJ Studies,* no. 23, 2016 edn (2014 data), 2016

Credit Suisse Research Institute, The CS Gender 3000: The Reward for Change, 2016

European Commission, Gender Balance on Corporate Boards: Europe is Cracking the Glass Ceiling, 2015

4. Health and Reproduction

Mahmoud F. Fathalla, 'Safe motherhood at twenty-five: Looking back, moving forward', video-recorded speech, London, 2012

World Health Organization (WHO) Constitution (45th edn, 2006)

Raoul Fransen dos Santos, World Health Organization Bulletin, vol. 87, no. 11, 2009

Sarah Hawkes, 'Investment case for eliminating mother-to-child transmission of syphilis: Promoting better maternal and child health and stronger health systems', WHO, 2012

United Nations Education, Scientific and Cultural Organization (UNESCO), Emerging Evidence, Lessons and Practice in Comprehensive Sexuality Education: A Global Review, 2015

Rose Zambezi and Juan Jacobo Hernandez, 'Engaging communities in youth reproductive health and HIV projects', 2011

HIV I-base (treatment activist group) – http://i-base.info/about-us/

Centers for Disease Control and Prevention (CDC), 'Youth risk behavior surveillance – United States, 2013', *Morbidity and Mortality Weekly Report,* 63 (4), 2014

Abby Young-Powell, 'Six of the best sex education programmes around the world', *Guardian,* 20 May 2017

The International Planned Parenthood Federation (IPPF), Annual Performance Report 2015–2016

Clue, 'Talking about periods – an international investigation', survey interactive map, 2015 – http://www.helloclue.com/survey.html

Reuters, 'Nepalese teenager dies after being banished to shed for menstruating', *Guardian,* 21 December 2016

Shanti Kadariya and Arja R. Aro, 'Chhaupadi practice in Nepal – analysis of ethical aspects', *Dove Press Journal: Medicolegal and Bioethics,* 2015

Lifting the Lid, film directed by Chella Quint, 2014

Chella Quint, 'Adventures in Menstruation', TEDx, 2012

Always, 'Check no stain' advert campaign, 2010–16

Always, '#Like a girl' advert, 2015

Bodyform, 'Blood' advert campaign, 2016

Pharie Sefali, 'I use a sock as a sanitary pad, says Langa learner', *GroundUp,* 6 November 2014

I, Daniel Blake, film directed by Ken Loach, 2017

IPPF, 'Sexual and reproductive health and rights – the key to gender equality and women's empowerment', 2015

Center for Reproductive Rights (CRR), 'Abortion worldwide: 20 years of reform', 2014

Amnesty International, 'She is not a criminal: The impact of Ireland's abortion law', 2015

Eighth Amendment of the Constitution (of Ireland) Act, 1983

Protection of Life During Pregnancy Act, 2013

United Nations Population Fund (UNFPA), Programme of Action: Adopted at the International Conference on Population and Development, Cairo, 5–13 September 1994, 2004

CRR, 'Whose right to life? Women's rights and prenatal protections under human rights and comparative law', 2014

CRR, The World's Abortion Laws 2014, map, 2014

United Nations (UN) Millennium Development Goals, 2000

UN, The Millennium Development Goals Report 2015, 2015

UN Sustainable Development Goals, 2016

UN, 2030 Agenda for Sustainable Development Goals, 2015

WHO, Improving Maternal Mental Health, 2008

WHO, Maternal Mental Health and Child Health and Development: Literature Review of Risk Factors and Interventions on Postpartum Depression, 2008

5. Home

United Nations (UN), Universal Declaration of Human Rights, 1948

UN, International Covenant on Economic, Social and Cultural Rights, 1966

UN, 'Report of the Special Rapporteur on adequate housing as a component of the right to an adequate standard of living, and on the right to non-discrimination in this context', UN

General Assembly, 71st session, Item 69(b) of the provisional agenda, 2016

Rights of Women, 'Domestic violence, housing and homelessness', 2012

Human Rights Watch, 'Double standards: Women's property rights violations in Kenya', 2003

Office of the United Nations High Commission for Human Rights (OHCHR) and UN Habitat, The Right to Adequate Housing, factsheet no. 21 (rev. 1), 2009

OHCHR, Women and the Right to Adequate Housing, 2012

Open Society, 'Securing women's land and property rights: A critical step to address HIV, violence, and food security', 2014

Heinrich Boll Foundation, 'Women and land rights: Questions of access, ownership and control', *Perspectives*, vol. 2, no. 13, 2013

Parliament of Sierra Leone, The Devolution of Estates Act, 2007

Republic of Rwanda, 'Matrimonial Regimes, Liberalities and Successions, Law no. 22/99, 1999

Constitution of Zambia Act, 2016

Constitution of the Republic of Botswana, 1966 (as amended up to 2006)

Constitution of the Republic of Uganda, 1995

Republic of Uganda, The Uganda National Land Policy, 2013

Human Rights Education Associates (HREA), The Moroccan Family Code (Moudawana), 2004

The Brookings Institute and the London School of Economics, A Year of Living Dangerously: A Review of Natural Disasters in 2010, 2011

Heather Stewart, 'Emily Thornberry accuses Chuka Umunna of virtue signalling on EU vote', *Guardian*, 30 June 2017

Germaine Greer, *The Female Eunuch*, 1970 (re-published by Fourth Estate, 2012)

The Organization for Economic Co-operation and Development (OECD), The ABC of Gender Equality in Education: Aptitude, Behaviour, Confidence, 2015

World Economic Forum, The Global Gender Gap Report 2015, 2015

United Nations Education, Scientific and Cultural Organization (UNESCO), Global Education Monitoring Report 2016, 2016

International Monetary Fund (IMF), World Economic Outlook, Update January 2017, 2017

Nadeem Malik, *Corporate Social Responsibility and Development in Pakistan* (Routledge, 2015)

Plan International (with Ipos MORI), 'Girls speak out: A four-country survey of young women's attitudes and recommendations for action', 2015

Street Child, Annual Report 2016, 2016

The White House, Office of the Press Secretary, Let Girls Learn – A Comprehensive Investment in Adolescent Girls' Education, factsheet, 2016

Girls' Education South Sudan (GESS), Annual Review 2015, 2015

The World Bank, Gender Data Portal: Education – http://data topics.worldbank.org/gender/topic/education

Lisa W. Foderaro, 'Yale restricts a fraternity for five years', *New York Times*, 17 May 2011

Aaron Benavot and Catherine Jere, 'Gender bias is rife in textbooks', Global Education Monitoring Report, *World Education* blog, 8 March 2016

UNESCO, Education for All 2000–2015: Achievements and Challenges, 2015

Janice McCabe, Emily Fairchild, Liz Grauerholz, Bernice A. Pescosolido and Daniel Tope, 'Gender in twentieth-century children's books: Patterns of disparity in titles and central characters', *SAGE Journals*, 2011

Tom McTague, 'June Eric-Udorie: Feminism to be taught in A Level politics curriculum after teenager's campaign', *Independent*, 9 January 2016

Hidden Figures, film directed by Theodore Melfi, 2017

7. Insecurity

Anthony Loyd, 'Niqabs thrown in the sand as women flee Raqqa', *The Times*, 8 May 2017

International Centre for Prison Studies (ICPS), World Female Imprisonment List (second edn, 2012)

ICPS, World Prison Population List (11th edn, 2011)

United Nations International Children's Emergency Fund (UNICEF), 2015

World Health Organization (WHO), Female Genital Mutilation, factsheet, 2017

United Nations Convention Against Torture and Other Cruel, Inhuman or Degrading Treatment or Punishment, 1984

United Nations Convention on the Elimination of All Forms of Discrimination Against Women (CEDAW), 1979

United Nations Convention on the Rights of the Child, 1989

Sue Lloyd-Roberts, *The War on Women* (Simon & Schuster, 2016)

World Economic Forum, The Horrors of Modern Slavery, in Numbers, 2016

The Global Slavery Index 2016 Report, 2016

United Nations Education, Scientific and Cultural Organization (UNESCO), 'School-related gender-based violence is preventing the achievement of quality education for all', 2015

UNICEF, 'Hidden in Plain Sight - a Statistical Analysis of Violence Against Children', 2014

European Union Agency for Fundamental Rights, Violence Against Women: An EU-wide Survey; Results at a Glance, 2014

UN, 'Violence against women', The World's Women, 2015

Law Commission, 'Rape within Marriage', working paper no. 118, 1990

R v C [1991] 1 All ER 755, House of Lords

R v R [1992] 1 A. C. 599, House of Lords

Council of Europe, Convention on Preventing and Combating Violence against Women and Domestic Violence' (Istanbul Convention), 2011

Rihanna and Diane Sawyer, ABC interview, 2009

WHO, 'Violence Against Women: Intimate Partner and Sexual Violence Against Women', factsheet, 2016

UN Women, Safe Cities Free from Violence Against Women and Girls: Baseline Findings from the 'Safe City Delhi Programme', 2012

United Nations High Commissioner for Refugees (UNHCR), Global Trends: Forced Displacement in 2015, 2016

WOMAN with Gloria Steinman (Season 1), Viceland documentary, 2016

Aristophanes, *Lysistrata,* 411 BC, translation by James Morrison (IMMEDIATE ARTS, 1981)

UN, Universal Declaration of Human Rights, 1948

8. Faith

Margaret Atwood, *The Handmaid's Tale* (McClelland & Stewart, 1985)

WIN-Gallup International, Global Index of Religiosity and Atheism, 2012

Mary Shelley, *Frankenstein* (Lackington, Hughes, Harding, Mavor & Jones, 1818)

Pope Francis, address to the Centro Italiano Femminile (Italian Women's Centre), 25 July 2014

Stephanie Kirchgaessner, 'Pope Francis says women will never be Roman Catholic priests', *Guardian*, 1 November 2016

Elaine Storkey, *Created or Constructed: The Great Gender Debate* (Paternoster Press, 2000)

Rachel Held Evans, *A Year of Biblical Womanhood* (Thomas Nelson, 2012)

Fatema Mernissi, *Beyond the Veil: Male-female Dynamics in Modern Muslim Society* (Saqi Books, 1975)

Fatema Mernissi, *The Veil and the Male Elite: A Feminist Interpretation of Women's Rights in Islam* (Basic Books, 1991)

Sayeeda Warsi, *The Enemy Within* (Allen Lane, 2017)

Susan Carland, *Fighting Hislam: Women, Faith and Sexism* (Melbourne University Press, 2017)

Shami Chakrabarti, *On Liberty* (Penguin, 2014)

Larry King, 'A female Dalai Lama?', Dalai Lama interview, Ora TV, 2014

Wotchit TV, 'Dalai Lama says if there is a female Dalai Lama in the future, she must be "attractive"', interview, 2015

Bhaji on the Beach, film directed by Gurinder Chadha, 1993

Bend It Like Beckham, film directed by Gurinder Chadha, 2002

Viceroy's House, film directed by Gurinder Chadha, 2017

Acknowledgements

I owe first thanks to my son for the tablet, the encouragement to write that came with it and all the heated debate and food for thought.

Tracy Bohan at the Wylie Agency believed in the project from before its inception. Thank you doesn't quite cut it for all the advice, support and laughter.

Enormous thanks to my wonderful editor Helen Conford and to Shoaib Rokadiya, Annabel Huxley, Richard Duguid and all the team at Allen Lane and Penguin for making this such a rewarding and stimulating experience. It was a privilege to be able to work with copy-editor Bela Cunha once more.

To my fearless feminist friends and readers Ellie Hobhouse, Rachel Holmes and Marie Claire Rodgers – so much gratitude for all the inspiration, input, discussion and solidarity.

Connie Kovats, thank you for your thoughts. I am so reassured that you represent the future of women in our world.

Thanks to Louise Raw for keeping the flame of the Matchwomen and so many more alive.

Andrea Coomber and Rachel Jones from JUSTICE provided vital information on comparative judicial diversity, as did Florence Burton and Jonathan Evans on wealth, Polly Clayden of HIV I-Base, Liz Campbell and BA on health. My old school friend Susan Palmer gave me a new take on school and what it might yet be.

Thanks to Karla McLaren and her colleagues at Amnesty International UK for the precious time and trouble they spared me and for the vital work that they do every day.

Never was the academy so kind, generous and unstuffy as

in the form of my three feminist professor friends: Janet Beer, Vice-Chancellor of the University of Liverpool, Anthony Forster of the University of Essex, and Joanne Conaghan, head of the Law School at the University of Bristol.

Katie Bales is a brilliant young law lecturer, also at the University of Bristol. Thanks for our great and stimulating chats that always left me thinking.

Amy Campbell Golding and Susan Mulholland at mystart. co.uk deserve more support and recognition for their groundbreaking work with refugees and school-aged children, as does Jaf Shah of Acid Survivors International (asti. org.uk) for his mission to end acid violence in the world.

Thanks to my friend and colleague Jan Royall for being so consistent in less than consistent times.

Thanks to Alison Foster QC, Deok Joo Rhee QC and all my learned friends at 39 Essex Chambers for the warmth of the professional environment they have nurtured.

Solidarity and respect to all the women and men of the United Kingdom Shadow Cabinet of 2016–17. It has been a privilege to share your values, mission and company. Particular thanks to my friends and colleagues Diane Abbott, Cat Smith and Emily Thornberry for the thoughts and conversations that we shared on the cause of women.